Gibraltar and Its People

Gibraltar
and Its People

PHILIP DENNIS

David & Charles
Newton Abbot   London

British Library Cataloguing in Publication Data

Dennis, Philip
   Gibraltar and Its People.
   1. Gibraltar, history
   I. Title
   946'.89

   ISBN 0–7153–9493–2

Printed in Great Britain
by Billings & Sons Ltd
for David & Charles Publishers plc
Brunel House   Newton Abbot   Devon

Contents

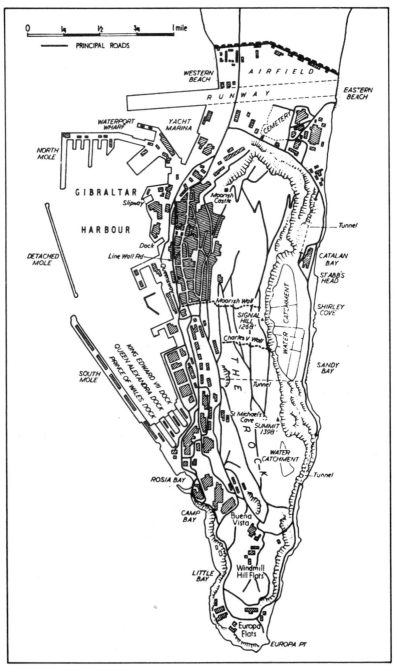

Sketch map of 'The Rock' based on that of Service Publications Ltd

1
The Rock

Few places as small as Gibraltar have so much history woven around them and attract as much attention today. In 1987 Spain delayed an EEC agreement on air fares by objecting to the inclusion of the airport at Gibraltar as a British airport. In March 1988 Gibraltar was the scene of an attempted bomb attack by the IRA, which was foiled by close British and Spanish co-operation. The latter was the fruit of long-standing friendly relations, but British possession of some 2¼ square miles of land at Gibraltar has been a source of contention for nearly three centuries. Spain still sees Gibraltar both as a jewel to be returned and a thorn in its side. Why is this the case after such a long time? Where do the Gibraltarians, whose home it is, stand in this Anglo-Spanish dispute? These questions can only be answered by looking at Gibraltar as it is today, in the light of the Rock's own history and contemporary events in the world at large.

First, the nature of the Rock of Gibraltar itself and its location between the Atlantic and the Mediterranean must be considered. These factors have played a great part in Gibraltar's history, and a description of the Rock as it has been seen by travellers in the past and as it appears today gives some guide to its part in history. The traditional approach from Britain was by sea through the Straits of Gibraltar from the west, when the Rock would appear out of the mist looking like a crouching lion guarding the Straits at the entrance to the Mediterranean. In former years the Rock epitomised British sea power, which stretched out east through a chain of bases to Hong Kong. Ocean liners no longer follow the sea route to the east through the Suez Canal, but travellers on cruise ships still get the same view. More usual approaches now are by road through Spain, or by air. From the hills south of Ronda in Andalusia, the Rock appears in the far distance as a prominent feature jutting out of the sea somewhat reminiscent of Portland Bill seen from the hills of Dorset; it is indeed composed of limestone of a similar Jurassic Age formed under water between 135 and 180 million years ago.

The air route from Britain to Gibraltar crosses the Spanish coast in the vicinity of Malaga, passing over the brown sandstone foothills south-west of the Sierra Nevada. The Rock appears as a much lighter coloured peninsula attached to the mainland by a low isthmus, which would be scarcely visible without the buildings on it. The whiteness of the limestone of the Rock is accentuated by the concrete-covered water catchments on the eastern side.

The best view from the air is obtained from a seat on the right-hand side of the aircraft when the landing on the isthmus runway is from the western side into an easterly wind. Then the aircraft circles right round the Rock, giving first a view of the precipitous northern cliff in which the mountain rises from 10ft above sea level to over 1,300ft. From there a sharp ridge stretches southwards to the highest point of the Rock standing near the southern end of the ridge at a height of 1,398ft above sea level. The Rock then descends in two steep steps; these are raised beaches representing former sea levels. The first steep descent is to Windmill Hill nearly 1,000ft below the summit. Below this the next step down is to Europa Flats at the southern end of the Rock just 100ft above sea level; this area in turn is surrounded by cliffs going down to the sea.

Along the whole of the eastern side of the Rock the slopes to the sea from the ridge forming the summit are very steep, so it is easy to see that defenders did not have to bother much about approaches from the eastern side. There are few habitations on this side apart from two hotels and the village of Catalan Bay; this was once a fishing village but now tourists are more lucrative than fish.

Before the aircraft approaching Gibraltar makes a right-hand turn south of the Rock, on a clear day there is a view across the Straits to Mt Abyla (known in Gibraltar as Apes' Hill). It stands out on the African shore as a rounded mountain and, together with Gibraltar, was known as one of the Pillars of Hercules in Roman times. In the foreground north of the mountain there is

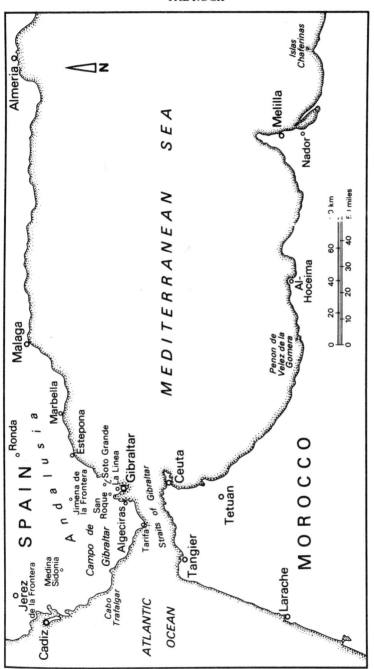

Spain, Morocco and Gibraltar

the peninsula and harbour of Ceuta; this is a Spanish enclave in North Africa surrounded by Moroccan territory. As the aircraft turns right there is a brief view westwards through the Straits of Gibraltar, with Tarifa Point visible on the Spanish shore beyond Carnero Point at the western end of the Bay of Gibraltar. Tarifa Point (Latitude 35° 59'N) is the most southerly point on the mainland of Europe; it is a few minutes of latitude south of Europa Point at the southern tip of the Rock. The whole area of the Straits, including the Atlas Mountains in North Africa, is part of a mountain system formed in the Tertiary Era, known as the Betic Cordillera. It is not known how the division of the Straits occurred, but a view westwards gives the impression of a very wide river between Africa and Europe; one theory is that the Straits were formed by a process of erosion brought about by changing sea levels.

As the aircraft approaches the southern tip of the Rock the lighthouse at Europa Point stands out prominently and the level ground around it can be clearly seen. This area is now used for military training and recreation. The lighthouse stands 61ft above ground level and gives a beam which can be seen for 30 miles in clear weather; it was completed in 1838.

Further north along the coast is the old harbour of Rosia Bay in which Nelson's flagship, the *Victory*, berthed after the Battle of Trafalgar with the great admiral's body on board. A more impressive sight, however, is the large naval harbour and dockyard further to the north covering some 440 acres of enclosed waters. This harbour is now partly in commercial use, as it is no longer needed for the large battle fleets of the two world wars, but it is still used by the smaller modern ships of British and NATO navies. Behind the harbour, rising in tiers up the Rock, are closely packed buildings. Many of Gibraltar's 30,000 inhabitants live in this area; just over 20,000 of the population are Gibraltarians and the rest include service personnel and persons engaged in commerce and industry temporarily resident in Gibraltar. Once again the view of the Rock as a whole shows its defensive strength, but landing on the west side was less difficult before the naval dockyard was built at the beginning of the twentieth century.

Before the dockyard existed, walls and fortifications had been built on the shales and sands overlying the limestone but, in Moorish times, landing on the sands was a frequent route for attack. The steep slopes behind the sands where the rugged limestone rises sharply gave great advantages to defenders, but it is an illusion to regard the limestone mountain as solid. Inside the mountain are many caves, eroded in the same manner as those in Somerset in Britain. Around the coasts, too, there are many sea caves. One of the caves eroded by the sea yielded human remains of Neanderthal Age and many other interesting discoveries have been made, including some of Phoenician origin. The Rock of Gibraltar is traditionally synonymous with strength; the term even passed into French where it has been used for instance to describe a lady who was an ardent preserver and restorer of historical monuments as *le Roc de Gibraltar des Monuments Historiques.*

Another feature which might be seen when an aircraft is circling the Rock before landing is a banner cloud around the summit. When the east wind blows off the Mediterranean, warm moist air is forced upwards and condenses as it cools, forming a cloud. At most seasons it is a fairly light cloud but in summer it can become dark and heavy, casting a shadow on the town and producing an oppressive atmosphere. The east wind is known as the Levanter and weather associated with it is often regarded as the cause of all ills.

When landing at Gibraltar Airport from the west, the aircraft touches down on a part of the 2,000-yard-long runway built out into the sea during World War II. The runway is adjacent to two yacht marinas, which have been developed in recent years and provide berthing accommodation for local and visiting yachtsmen. The sheer cliff of the north face of the Rock is an impressive sight, which can only be viewed with awe by rock climbers. It has been scaled on a number of occasions but few climbers will feel inclined to go further than speculating upon possible routes.

If the approach to Gibraltar by air is much more interesting than that to most airports, the airport buildings themselves are unspectacular. Designed at a time when fewer people travelled by air, the buildings are too cramped for present requirements.

11

However, the impression given by staff dealing with immigration, baggage handling and customs is one of courteous efficiency; this is something generally met throughout Gibraltar.

The airport buildings are adjacent to the Spanish frontier, about ½ mile from the town and just over 3 miles from Europa Point. A visitor from Britain will have travelled over 1,200 miles since leaving home, having moved southwards through about 15 degrees of latitude to 36° 7'N. The longitude of 5° 21'W is about the same as Cape Wrath (north-west Scotland) and The Lizard (south-west England). The change in latitude can usually be detected in a change of temperature; Gibraltar can generally be expected to be about 15°F warmer in winter and about 10°F warmer in summer. In winter, however, it can rain heavily, particularly between November and January, when about half the average annual rainfall of 32 inches can be expected.

Looking towards the Rock from the airport buildings, the daunting nature of the Rock for attackers from the isthmus can be felt. The sand is now covered with concrete and there are housing estates just north of the Rock built after World War II; these are partly on land previously covered by a defensive inundation. Behind this are ancient walls and battlements, with the keep of the Moorish Castle standing out prominently. Immediately north of the airport the road crosses the Spanish frontier. It is now a busy highway, but it was a very quiet area for thirteen years between 1969 and 1982 when it was closed to pedestrians as well as to motor traffic; the closure to motor traffic was imposed in October 1966 and lasted until February 1985.

There are two entrances to the town of Gibraltar from the north, one for pedestrians through the old Landport Gate and the other for traffic through Waterport Gates, which were the usual entry points in the days of sea travel. Main Street, the main artery of the town, is a narrow street about ¾ mile long containing a wide variety of shops, offices, banks, restaurants and other buildings. Modern shop fronts stand out in marked contrast to older buildings with louvred windows and Spanish-style tiles. Traffic is necessarily slow moving and often disrupted by building work when reconstruction and renovation become necessary in the old street. The British style of telephone booths, post boxes and taverns contrast with open-fronted Indian stores catering for the tourist trade. The police station just off Main Street is Victorian in style and houses a force indistinguishable from British bobbies. Their command of English is impeccable, as are their manners in dealing with requests for help, but amongst themselves they will often talk in Spanish. Like many Gibraltarians they are completely bilingual and switch easily from one language to the other, dependent upon which happens to be the more expressive in any particular instance. The human scene in the town is one of considerable activity and the differing styles of dress are as noticeable as the styles of buildings. There are well-dressed businessmen, bankers and civil servants, smartly attired Gibraltarian ladies, pram-pushing wives of British servicemen, long-robed Moroccan men and occasionally a Moroccan lady complete with yashmak, the latter contrasting sharply with the scanty dress of some tourists.

Many books have been written about the wars and sieges of Gibraltar's long history. There are also detailed books which deal with certain aspects of the Rock's natural history. An earlier book by the present writer deals with most of many aspects of environment and history in a correlative way. The purpose now, however, is to concentrate on those parts of Gibraltar's history which are particularly relevant to the present day, and to discuss the future of this interesting and pleasant place at the southern end of the mainland of Europe and the EEC.

At present Gibraltar is a British colony attached to the Spanish mainland. This is hurtful to Spanish pride and indeed it is stange to have a colony in Europe when many less well-developed places have become self-governing. In Africa the process began in 1957 with Ghana, a country about the same size as the United Kingdom. However, Pacific Islands like Nauru with a population of 7,300 and Tuvalu with 8,000 have also become independent in more recent years. For Gibraltar size is not a major problem, but Spanish aspiration to sovereignty is an obstacle to self-determination and independence, or whatever Gibraltarians may wish. The Spanish wish to regain sovereignty has existed ever since Gibraltar was captured by British and allied forces in 1704. The Rock was later ceded to Britain by the Treaty

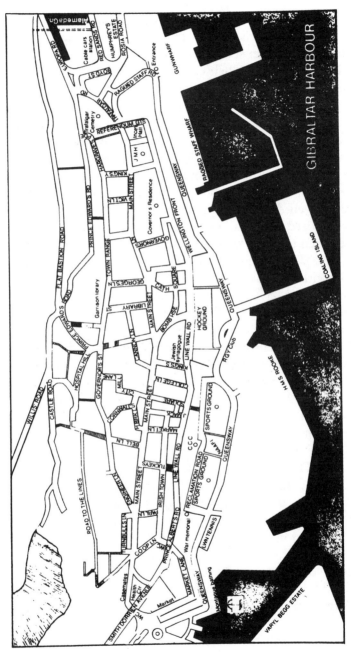

Town Street Plan

of Utrecht in 1713, which was regarded by Spain only as a temporary measure.

Spanish attention has recently been focused on events in the Falkland Islands and Hong Kong. In the former case Argentina, a Spanish-speaking South American country under the rule of a dictator much less wise than Franco, failed to take the islands by force. At that time (in 1982) Spain had been democratically governed for about five years, but there was considerable support for the Argentinian case. Hong Kong is rather different in that here Britain negotiated a return of the colony to Chinese rule in 1997. This was virtually inevitable as most of the land surface of the present British territory was only leased to Britain until 1997. Whilst these cases will be examined later it is also relevant to consider the Spanish enclaves of Ceuta and Melilla in North Africa and also small states in Europe such as Andorra and San Marino.

Although Gibraltar was known to the Phoenicians as well as the Romans, for present day purposes it is the Moorish history of Gibraltar that needs to be considered first. This began over twelve and a half centuries ago, but it is still important, as the Rock became a symbol of Moorish domination over the Spanish mainland. Gibraltar was in their hands for seven and a half centuries, in what in effect was a colonial situation.

2
Gebel Tarik

The first Moorish commander to use Gibraltar as a foothold in Europe was Tarik ibn Zeyad. The name Gibraltar is thought to have come about as a corruption of Gebel Tarik meaning Tarik's Mountain, but the origin is not absolutely certain.

There is some disagreement amongst historians about whether Tarik actually landed on the Rock of Gibraltar. There appears however to have been an attempted landing at some point elsewhere on the coast followed by a successful landing at or near Gibraltar; some 500 horsemen and 7,000 foot soldiers were then put ashore on a succession of nights in April 711. The Rock would have had unrivalled advantages as a bridgehead with great defensive strength. On the other hand there would have been a problem in finding water for such a large number of men and horses. There might, however, have been a surface stream which has since disappeared underground, as has happened in limestone districts in Britain and elsewhere. How water was obtained is a key question in establishing whether the actual landing was on the Rock, but in any event it seems clear that the Rock played its part as a good defensive site at least soon after the Moorish landing.

There was apparently little, if any, effort to dislodge Tarik's forces from the Rock and relatively minor defensive works were constructed at that time. There was a rapid advance inland and in July King Roderick's Visigoth forces were defeated in the Plain of Xeres in a battle in which he was killed. To some extent the war was a dispute amongst the Christian Visigoths as Count Julian, who was in control in Ceuta in North Africa, was using the invasion to pursue his own ambitions against Roderick; the quarrel with Roderick was heightened by an alleged seduction of Julian's daughter. The war soon escalated, acting as a stepping-stone to Moorish domination of mainland Spain. The Rock's role in this domination was thus considerable, and to this day Gibraltar is symbolic of the domination in Spanish minds.

ACTION AFTER FOUR CENTURIES

Very little happened in or around Gibraltar for over four centuries, but by the twelfth century the Castilian kings were having some successes against the Moors. This led to some fortifications being built on the Rock and the Moorish Wall still visible today overlooking the Red Sands (now the site of the Alameda Gardens) formed part of the fortifications ordered by Al-Mu'min in 1160. The keep of the castle still standing at the north end of the Rock was about two centuries later in construction, but there was an earlier keep on the same site.

During the thirteenth century the Moorish kingdom was in retreat before onslaughts by Castilian kings. Tarifa, Algeciras and Gibraltar became three strong points for the Moors, but Tarifa was lost by them in 1292. In 1309 Ferdinand IV of Castile set out to take Algeciras, but when the winter set in with heavy rains he changed his objective to Gibraltar; it was taken after a siege lasting a month. The Moors unsuccessfully besieged the Rock in 1316, but they were successful in the Rock's third siege in 1333; they were thus back in possession after only twenty-four years.

Alfonso XI of Castile arrived before the Rock later in 1333 and tried to recapture it but failed. Sixteen years later he commanded the fifth siege of the Rock and obtained naval help from Aragon in a siege lasting eight months. At the time the Black Death was ravaging much of Europe and this plague attacked Alfonso's forces, resulting in his death in 1350; his strong personal leadership was lost and the siege was raised.

The fourteenth and fifteenth centuries were marked by growing cohesion amongst the Castilians at least in so far as the Moors were concerned. This coincided with increasing quarrels amongst the Moors themselves and in 1411 the sixth siege marked one such quarrel. An earlier internal revolt had resulted in forces loyal to the King of Fez taking command of the Rock, but Yusof III of Granada re-established his authority in 1411 after a short siege.

In 1436 Henry de Guzman, Count of Niebla, made an attempt to capture the Rock in order to protect his estates between Tarifa and Cadiz from depredations by the Moors. He was unsuccessful and after he was drowned trying to land on the Red Sands, the Moors hung his body from the walls of the town; this proved a sufficient deterrent against further attack by forces on the isthmus.

The year 1462 stands out in Spanish history as the one which saw the end of Moorish domination of Gibraltar. Apart from a short period at the beginning of the fourteenth century, Gibraltar was in Moorish hands for the period from 711 to 1462, making them overlords for a total of over 700 years.

The recapture in 1462 is generally credited to action by Alonso de Arcos, who moved quickly from Tarifa with 250 men when he heard the garrison was temporarily weakened. He had, however, to await reinforcements from Medina Sidonia and there was fierce fighting before the Rock was taken. Thereafter, much argument ensued about feudal protocol before it was eventually agreed that the Duke of Medina should have possession of the Rock. In Spanish history, however, the tomb of Alonso in Seville gives him the credit for the recapture of Gibraltar on St Bernard's Day; St Bernard is still the patron saint.

GIBRALTAR UNDER SPANISH SOVEREIGNS

The Duke of Medina considered the Rock to be his by right after its capture, but Henry IV of Castile had other ideas and annexed it to his kingdom. The Duke gave it up under protest but began the ninth siege in 1466 and the castle was surrendered to him in 1467, fifteen months later. Peace was made with Henry IV which established Gibraltar as being within the territorial jurisdiction of the Duke of Medina.

An event of great importance in 1469 was the marriage between Ferdinand of Aragon and Isabella of Castile. Isabella succeeded to the throne of Castile in 1474 and Ferdinand to that of Aragon in 1479. Isabella confirmed the Duke of Medina as Marquis of Gibraltar, but after his death in 1492, she sought its surrender to her. The new Duke protested and only finally agreed to surrender Gibraltar in January 1502. A Royal Coat of Arms was granted to the city and is still retained.

Isabella's death in 1504 led to the Duke of Medina making another attempt to regain Gibraltar by means of a blockade in 1506, which is now known as the tenth siege. It was, however, abandoned without serious fighting. Ferdinand was appointed as Regent under Isabella's will for her daughter Joanna, and he thus held title to Gibraltar amongst his other offices until his death in 1516. He was succeeded by Joanna's son Charles V of the Holy Roman Empire, who became Charles I of Spain.

The Moorish kingdom of Granada continued for some years after the loss of the Rock in 1462, but even after the fall of Granada itself in 1492, there were still many Moorish residents who remained in Spain. They were closely associated with commerce but they were regarded with great disfavour by the Church, which sought to expel them and also Moroccan Jews. There was not, however, a Royal Decree to expel the Moors until one was issued by Philip III in 1609.

When Charles V of the Holy Roman Empire succeeded to the Spanish throne some half a century after the Spanish capture of the Rock in 1462, it was thought prudent to order a strengthening of the defences. Gibraltar had come to be seen as a symbol of victory over the Moors and was assuming a status as part of Spain as opposed to part of a Dukedom. There was considerable consternation in 1540 when Turkish pirates made a successful raid, and this led to the building of the Charles V Wall designed to protect the town from attack from the south where the Turks had landed apparently unobserved.

A royal visit to Gibraltar was made by Philip IV in 1624, which was followed by a further strengthening of defences. This included placing batteries at the southern end of the Rock and along the western seaboard and also a rebuilding of the northern defences. A new Landport Gate was built, as the previous one had displeased Philip IV in being too narrow for his carriage. Luis Bravo, the governor, had pointed out the advantages in keeping out enemies but this did not please the royal visitor.

RELATIONS BETWEEN ENGLAND AND SPAIN

Whilst Spain was becoming a pillar of the Holy Roman Empire during the sixteenth century, there were moves in Britain away from the Roman Catholic Church. The century started well for relationships between Britain and Spain with the marriage of Henry VIII to Catherine of Aragon in 1509, the year he ascended the throne. Catherine had been married to Henry's elder brother, who had died, but a papal dispensation was granted for the later marriage to Henry. No such dispensation was, however, obtainable for Henry's later wish for a divorce when the City of Rome was in the hands of Charles V, Catherine's nephew. This led to Henry moving away from Rome and dismissing his Cardinal, Wolsey. With the aid of the Reformation Parliament of 1529–36 he made himself Supreme Head of the Church of England.

When Mary, daughter of Catherine of Aragon, came to the English throne in 1553 and married Philip II of Spain there was an improvement in relations with Spain, at least at the highest level. There was, however, considerable opposition in England to the marriage and the return to Catholicism. The whole process was reversed when Elizabeth I, daughter of Anne Boleyn, came to the throne in 1558. Not only was there a return to Protestantism but English seamen, including Sir Francis Drake, openly buccaneered against Spanish shipping; it was called privateering.

The Spanish Armada sailed to the British shores in 1588 in the hope of invading the country and bringing about a return to the Catholic fold. As is well known, storms, the seamanship of the English and their ability to operate on short lines of communication frustrated a project which had been unlikely to succeed.

These events were far removed from Gibraltar but they were part of English and Spanish rivalry at sea. They led to Spanish awareness of vulnerability from the English and others, including the Dutch, and by 1627 Gibraltar was one of the most strongly fortified places around the Spanish coast. Charles I of England had ideas of action against Spain but he had so much trouble at home that any such ideas were abandoned.

Later Oliver Cromwell paid some attention to Gibraltar but no definite moves were made.

When Charles II of England married Catherine of Braganza, her dowry included the port of Tangier, which Portugal ceded to Britain. This was a useful base on the sea route around the Cape of Good Hope but it was given up in 1684, as Parliament refused to vote funds for its retention. It would have been useful in 1689 and later when England, Spain, the Netherlands, Bavaria and other German states were involved in the War of the League of Augsburg against France. In 1693 action took place around and near Gibraltar when Admiral Sir George Rooke had to disperse a convoy he was escorting to Mediterranean ports; some of the ships made their way to Gibraltar which the French attacked with fire ships. British crews improvised defences from the harbour mole at Gibraltar and saved their ships from heavy damage.

The war ended with the Peace of Ryswick in 1697. This resulted in France giving up parts of Catalonia, which had been taken from Spain earlier in the century, and in the recognition of William of Orange as King of England. He had deposed James II in 1688 and recognition by France was a step towards peace, but there was war again within a few years.

3
Britain, Spain and the Rock

The eighteenth century opened with the Bourbon King Louis XIV still at the height of his power in France; his motto *'L'Etat c'est moi'* typified his regime and he had great ambitions to dominate Europe. As far as Spain was concerned the British interest was in the succession of the Hapsburg Archduke Charles of Austria to the Spanish throne on the death of the ailing Charles II to prevent French hegemony and damage to British trade. However, under his will Charles II, who died during the year 1700, appointed Philip V to succeed him contrary to the Partition Treaties. Although Louis XIV had agreed to the Partition Treaties, he decided to recognise his grandson, Philip V, with a view to the possible union of the two thrones of France and Spain. In 1701 Louis made war with England even more inevitable by recognising James III, the Old Pretender, as King of England on the death of James II in exile in France. Apart from wishing to keep France and Spain apart, trade in the Mediterranean was an important British interest and ports such as Gibraltar, Ceuta and Oran in North Africa and Mahon in Minorca assumed strategic significance.

THE WAR OF THE SPANISH SUCCESSION
The War of the Spanish Succession began in 1702 after Queen Anne had succeeded to the English throne just a few years before the Act of Union with Scotland in 1707; this gave legislative effect to the unity of the crowns which had applied since 1603. The war was thus waged by a united Britain with its Dutch and Austrian allies. Land battles such as those at Blenheim (1704), Ramilies (1706), Oudenarde (1708) and Malplaquet (1709) stand out in history and resulted in severe damage to French land forces. The main task of the British naval forces, however, was to establish

the Archduke Charles on the Spanish mainland and to destroy the French fleet. Queen Anne had instructed Admiral Rooke to put himself under the command of the Archduke, whom he took to Lisbon in February 1704. Rooke sailed from there with troops under the command of Prince George of Hesse to Barcelona, where a Catalonian uprising was expected in favour of the Archduke becoming Charles III of Spain. There was no such uprising and Rooke was also unsuccessful in his secondary objective of finding and destroying the French fleet.

By July 1704 there had not been any progress towards winning the war at sea, so after a council of war on Rooke's flagship the *Royal Catherine* off Tetuan, it was decided to make an attack on Gibraltar to establish it as a base for Charles III. On 1 August about 2,000 marines from some fifty ships were put ashore on the isthmus. The Governor Don Diego Salinas was invited to surrender, but replied that the people of Gibraltar had sworn allegiance to Philip V.

An east wind kept the fleet away from the Rock for the next day, but the assault was resumed on 3 August. The main features of the assault were a very heavy bombardment lasting some six hours followed by a landing on the mole standing on the site of the present South Mole. An explosion of a magazine caused heavy casualties amongst the landing party, but Captains Hicks, Whittaker and Jumper distinguished themselves; the latter has a bastion named after him. Some historians think his name was Juniper, but his name has lived as Jumper in Gibraltar.

The women and children inhabitants of the Rock took refuge near Europa Point and became separated from the garrison in the town as a result of the landing. Fears for their safety and the general inadequacy of the defences led to surrender on 4 August. The surrender was taken by Prince George of Hesse, who was in command of the land forces in this allied operation, and the Rock was declared to be under the sovereignty of Charles III. The garrison were allowed to march out with three guns, some ammunition and provisions for six days. Civilians were allowed to remain, if they were prepared to swear allegiance to Charles III, but they nearly all took refuge in adjacent Spanish towns; the city's documents were taken to San Roque where some descendants of the former population are still thought to live.

Shortly after Gibraltar had been taken in the eleventh siege in the name of Charles III, its recapture was ordered by Philip V. Rooke's fleet had mostly left before the twelfth siege began, as many ships needed a refit after an indecisive battle with the French off Malaga. The expenditure of 15,000 rounds of ammunition in the capture of Gibraltar left Rooke's ships without enough ammunition for the battle and partly contributed to the failure to destroy the French fleet. It was not until 101 years later that the French fleet ceased to be a major force in the western Mediterranean; this was then the result of their defeat at Trafalgar.

The twelfth siege, begun in October 1704, nearly succeeded in an overnight attack led by a goatherd on a path he knew up the eastern side of the Rock. However, the attack was not followed up and Admiral Leake, left behind by Rooke with twenty ships, prevented the French fleet from invading from the sea. Amidst much argument between French and Spanish participants over the fault for the failure of the siege, it was abandoned early in 1705. Before the siege ended Philip V had replaced his own Spanish commander with Marshal Tesse, a Frenchman; this was an appropriate act in a war essentially one between Britain and her allies against France.

From 1704 until the Treaty of Utrecht in 1713 the Rock was occupied by British and allied forces on behalf of Charles III of Spain. There were stories of Rooke having ordered the British flag to be hoisted to declare the Rock British, but it seems more probable that any flags hoisted were used as markers in the course of the attack in 1704 to show where troops were situated for the purpose of directing fire.

From 1705 onwards consideration was given by British politicians, particularly the Tories, to seeking to keep Gibraltar as part of a deal for ending the war. The army and the navy were opposed to this, as the Rock was easily bombarded from land and sea and the prevalence of east or

west winds with sudden changes caused navigational difficulties.

THE TREATY OF UTRECHT

The Tories were in power when the Treaty of Utrecht was
drawn up to end a war which had proved expensive to all parties
and disastrous for the French army. It was agreed that Gibraltar
would be ceded to Britain as part of the treaty signed in 1713.
From the viewpoint of Louis XIV it was a way of ending the
war at Spanish expense. He had, however, established Philip V
on the throne of Spain and at least maintained his army and his
fleet in being, although both had suffered damage. From Philip's
point of view he was glad to be established on the throne and
seems to have thought Gibraltar recoverable by diplomacy or
war at an opportune time; Isabella's testamentary instruction
that Gibraltar should be kept Spanish in perpetuity was at least
temporarily being disregarded.

The Treaty itself ceded the town, castle, port and fortifications
to the Crown of Great Britain, 'to be held and enjoyed absolutely
with all manner of rights for ever, without any exception or
impediment whatsoever'. The full text of Article X of the Treaty
is quoted in Appendix 2. The Article can hardly be regarded as
drafted with geographical or legal precision; this may have been
necessary to make it acceptable on all sides. Certain points have
led to disputes over the centuries, but the draftsmen could hardly
have expected these points still to be in dispute 275 years later.

The first contentious clause reads: 'But that abuses and
frauds may be avoided by importing any kinds of goods,
the Catholic King wills and takes it to be understood, that
the above named propriety be yielded to Britain without any
territorial jurisdiction and without any open communication
by land with the country round about.' The Article goes on to
state that the provision regarding communication by land was
designed to prevent 'fraudulent importations of goods'. Jews
and Moors were to be excluded from Gibraltar which was in
keeping with discrimination against them in Spain. The Article
ends with a provision: 'And in case it shall hereafter seem meet
to the Crown of Great Britain to grant, sell, or by any means to

alienate therefrom the propriety of the said town of Gibraltar, it is hereby agreed, and concluded, that the preference of having the same shall always be given to the Crown of Spain before any others.' This last sentence has been a source of friction in recent times. The Gibraltar Constitution of 1969 was stated by Spain to be an infringement on the grounds that it gave power to Gibraltarians in setting up the Gibraltar House of Assembly.

Perhaps the most contentious point has been the question of territorial jurisdiction. The exclusion of territorial jurisdiction clearly prevented any possible British claim to the Campo de Gibraltar as the area around Gibraltar was known at the time of the treaty. There remains the problem of where the boundary of British sovereign territory stands. Britain claims that it always had rights over the isthmus under the custom of jurisdiction extending to a cannon-ball shot from a fort or castle. Spain claims that this privilege, generally regarded as being a distance of 1,000 yards, was excluded by the reference to territorial jurisdiction.

There were no particular rights of land communication with Spain conferred by the treaty except for a provision that in case of need 'it may be lawful to purchase, for ready money, in the neighbouring territories of Spain provisions and other things necessary for the use of the garrison, the inhabitants and the ships which lie in the harbour'. In practice the frontier has been freely crossed at all times except when sieges have been in progress, or when there has been a closure such as that imposed by General Franco's government in 1969.

The use of land on the isthmus has been the practice of the garrison since early in the nineteenth century, but the erection of a fence in 1908 led to a protest. Spain now claims that the airport and other installations on the isthmus are on Spanish territory.

DIPLOMACY FOLLOWED BY WAR

In 1714, the year after the Treaty of Utrecht, George I came to the throne in Britain. Both he and his Secretary of State, the Earl of Stanhope, favoured giving up Gibraltar in return for concessions from Spain. Louis XIV died in 1715 and Philip V set about improving Spanish military power to offset the previous reliance on France. He was aware of the views of

George I regarding Gibraltar but rejected an offer in 1721 of an exchange for Florida or some other territory overseas. Later in the year George I offered – without mention of an exchange – to put the restoration of Gibraltar before Parliament for approval. In Spain the letter proposing this became known as 'King George's promise'. The British view was that the letter expressed nothing more than a personal willingness on the part of George I. He had in fact the theoretical right to act under the royal prerogative in such matters, but in practice he could not have done so against the will of Parliament. Philip V probably did not appreciate how far the Revolution of 1688 and the Act of Settlement of 1701 had weakened the position of the monarch. George I was only moderately secure on his throne and understandably he wanted good relations with Philip V; a Jacobite revival supported by the 'Catholic King' was still a possibility in Britain.

These and other diplomatic exchanges did not produce any positive results. Lord Townshend, who succeeded the Earl of Stanhope in 1721, held different views over Gibraltar. He favoured Britain's retention of the Rock, and chose not to see a favourable opportunity to put its restoration to Spain before Parliament. By 1726 war had become inevitable. Charles VI of Austria, who had failed to become Charles III of Spain, played a part in this by secretly agreeing to support the return of Gibraltar to Spain.

When Spanish forces started gathering around the Rock at the end of 1726 the defences were not in very good repair and only 1,500 men were in the garrison. A well led surprise attack might have succeeded, but instead some 15,000 men were mustered under the Count de las Torres, whilst reinforcements came to the Rock. Some of these were from Minorca which had also been ceded to Britain under the Treaty of Utrecht. Others came from Britain in April 1727 with the Governor Lord Portmore, who returned to his post; leaving the Rock under a deputy was common practice at the time.

The garrison of the Rock was built up to over 5,000 men, but numbers were not particularly relevant, as it was mainly a gunners' battle between the 200 or so guns on each side. The Spanish guns after providing a heavy bombardment suffered from droop in their barrels or blew up. British command of the seas was also important as it enabled reinforcements to land at the south end of the Rock out of range of Spanish guns. Some damage to Spanish forces on the isthmus was caused by enfilade fire from the sea.

The siege ended with a truce in June 1727, but there were long peace negotiations thereafter leading to the Treaty of Seville in November 1729. Philip V was a sick man at the time of the negotiations, but his second wife Elizabeth Farnese played an important part in delaying a Treaty. Her attitude changed when it was agreed that her son Charles should have Parma and Tuscany. Eventually the Treaty of Seville did not specifically mention Gibraltar, but confirmed the Treaty of Utrecht.

Whilst negotiations were in progress Britain asked Spanish troops to withdraw 1,000 yards away from the Rock according to custom. The Spanish troops withdrew, but claimed that they did so only as a gesture of goodwill. There was, however, little goodwill at this time between Britain and Spain over Gibraltar. The period between the Treaty of Utrecht and the Treaty of Seville did great harm to relations between the two countries. The Spanish feeling that Britain had acted in bad faith after 'King George's promise' was exacerbated by a military defeat.

The Treaty of Utrecht was once again confirmed without specific reference to Gibraltar in the Treaty of Aix-la-Chapelle, which ended the War of the Austrian Succession in 1748. The Seven Years War (1756–63) did not greatly affect Gibraltar and left its status unchanged. The island of Minorca, however, was in the forefront. It had been British since 1713 but the French took the island from Britain in 1756 after Admiral Byng, whose father was present at the capture of Gibraltar, withdrew his fleet to avoid superior French forces. He was subsequently acquitted of cowardice, but found guilty of failing to do his utmost against the enemy. This also carried the death penalty and thus gave rise to Voltaire's famous words: 'Dans ce pays-ci il est bon de tuer de temps en temps un amiral pour encourager les autres.' History should, however, perhaps be kinder to Admiral Byng. His fleet would have suffered almost certain disaster had he not withdrawn and this would also have left Gibraltar open to attack.

In the course of the Seven Years War the case of Gibraltar did come into question, with the possibility of surrendering it to Spain being considered in return for help from Spain in recovering Minorca. However, nothing came of this and Minorca was returned to Britain under the Peace of Paris in 1763; once again Spanish hopes were unfulfilled.

THE GREAT SIEGE 1779–83

The Great Siege itself has been described in detail by Captain John Drinkwater in *A History of the Late Siege* published in 1785. Drinkwater was present at the siege and many later writers have gone into detail on the subject. The important factor to consider here is the set-back suffered once again by Spanish armed forces. This time a well prepared and long campaign was frustrated.

In the years following the Peace of Paris in 1763 Britain had few friends in Europe, and the North American colonies were restive. Charles III of Spain, who succeeded Ferdinand IV in 1759, was watching for an opportunity to recover the Rock. As a son of Elizabeth Farnese, the second wife of Philip V, he probably acquired her dislike of the British at an early age.

For their part the British were not idle in Gibraltar after the end of the Seven Years War. Two people who played a great part in putting the Rock's defences in good shape were Colonel Green who arrived in 1761 and General Eliott who was appointed Governor in 1776. Colonel Green was a gunner and engineer who patiently supervised the building of gun emplacements and the siting of guns. General Eliott was a Scot educated in Edinburgh and the University of Leyden in Holland. He spoke French and German fluently and had served in the German army as well as the British army. He distinguished himself in the Seven Years War in which he tried hard to prevent the common custom of indiscriminate plunder. He was just the strong, austere leader who was needed to withstand siege.

Until June 1779 – when the frontier was closed after the breaking of relations between Britain and Spain – General Eliott maintained good personal relations with General Mendoza, who was in charge of the Spanish forces. His last visit on 19 June just before General Mendoza left to take up a new post must have been embarrassing as Mendoza knew war was imminent whereas Eliott had not yet been informed.

Nothing much happened until September, but the Spanish navy was imposing an increasing blockade. The British navy was greatly stretched at the time through having to maintain forces in North America as well as watch the French and Spanish fleets in European waters. After several frustrating months General Eliott decided that something should be done and opened a bombardment of the Spanish lines with the order 'Britons strike home'. To boost civilian morale he arranged for the wife of a member of the garrison to fire the first shot, but there was not much return of fire from the Spanish lines. By the end of the year, the biggest problem had become the shortage of food.

In January 1780 the situation was saved by the arrival of a convoy under Admiral Rodney. He had served with distinction in earlier wars of the eighteenth century and was on his way to take up a command in the West Indies. He skilfully evaded the French fleet off Brest and later defeated a Spanish naval force off Cape St Vincent. The Commander Admiral Juan de Langara was captured and taken as a prisoner of war to Gibraltar. Before his return to Spain in an exchange of prisoners of war de Langara found Prince William, a son of George III and later King William IV, serving as a midshipman. He expressed surprise, saying, 'Well does Britain merit the empire of the sea when the humblest stations in her navy are supported by Princes of the Blood'. Two centuries later the Spanish-speaking Argentinians may have also been surprised by Prince Andrew serving off the Falkland Islands as a junior naval officer.

During 1780 occasional supplies reached the Rock from Morocco, but at the end of the year the Emperor, Mahomed I, decided to give support to Spain, so the situation in Gibraltar again became critical through lack of food. A convoy of ships arrived under Admiral Darby in April 1781 bringing flour, other food supplies and ammunition, thus saving the situation. There was a heavy bombardment as the ships unloaded, but by unloading at the southern end of the

Rock they managed to keep out of range of the Spanish guns.

By the autumn of 1781 the Spanish lines on the isthmus were seen to be being pushed forward towards the Rock. This caused General Eliott and General Boyd, his second in command, to plan a sortie to destroy some of the Spanish works. This took place on 27 November when about 2,000 men moved onto the isthmus under General Ross. The raid was most successful and about the only deviation from plan was the arrival of Eliott himself on the scene towards the end of the operation; he did not have the temperament required to remain at his headquarters whilst the battle was elsewhere.

The fourteenth siege of Gibraltar reached its climax in 1782. The Spaniards planned an attack by land and sea preceded by a heavy bombardment. The attack from the sea was by ships specially prepared with wet sand and wet cork between the timbers to prevent splintering and with a system of pipes to sprinkle water to put out fires caused by red hot shot. However, this primitive form of sprinkler system did not work and by the end of the day of the attack, 13 September, the bay was lit up by burning ships. Characteristically Eliott made his headquarters in King's Bastion the centre of the defences. For Spain the day was a major disaster. There had been much publicity given to this final attack and it was watched by many from hills around the Rock; for them the burning ships was a sorry sight which must have deeply hurt Spanish pride.

The blockade continued after the failure of the September assault, but a third large relieving fleet came in October under Lord Howe. Hostilities were finally ended on 3 February 1783, in triumph for the garrison under General Eliott, who later became the first Lord Heathfield; he had shown himself both a great leader and a competent planner. He disciplined himself as well as his troops and proved he could live on four ounces of rice a day for a week. He was also receptive to ideas. In the earliest days of the siege it was found necessary to produce air bursts from shells to stop their effect being masked by the sand of the isthmus. An infantryman, Captain Mercier, solved the problem of how to set shorter fuses. At the time a Lieutenant

Shrapnel was a member of the garrison and almost certainly was influenced by these events in the later development of the ammunition named after him.

Another gunnery problem solved during the siege was how to fire from high up on the Rock at an angle of depression. For this purpose Lieutenant Koehler designed a gun carriage, the forerunner of much later recoil systems. A model can be seen in the Gibraltar Museum. The most remarkable piece of work during the siege was the tunnelling into the Rock for the purpose of getting a gun to a point from which fire could be brought to bear on the Mediterranean shore. This was the idea of Sergeant Ince and in the course of tunnelling it was found that air holes through the North face were necessary. These made excellent sites for guns and by the end of the siege four guns had been mounted.

The weight of numbers and artillery during the siege was heavily on the Spanish side. Spanish and French forces amounted at one time to over 40,000 men and there were 246 guns on the isthmus taking part in the bombardment in September 1782. The British forces during the siege numbered between 5,500 and 7,000 men and only 96 serviceable guns. Superiority in numbers was not however a big advantage, as deployment could only be on a narrow front and the administration required was a disadvantage. The only really effective weapon available to the Spanish forces was blockade and this on occasions was not far from being successful.

THE END OF THE EIGHTEENTH CENTURY

Charles III of Spain had set his heart upon recovering Gibraltar, but failed. This must have been as big a blow as the loss of Calais to Britain in Queen Mary's reign two centuries earlier. Charles III died in 1788 and was succeeded by Charles IV. In the next year the French Revolution set the pattern for events in Europe for the next twenty-five years. Britain and Spain came together in war against France in 1793, but Spain changed sides in 1796 after peace was made with France. This resulted in a heavy defeat for the Spanish fleet off Cape St Vincent in 1797 and the loss of Minorca in 1798; these events greatly reduced any threat to Gibraltar and there was no repetition of the earlier sieges.

The eighteenth century had an effect on relations between Britain and Spain which is still strongly felt today. Gibraltar was taken in the name of the Archduke Charles in the eleventh siege in 1704 when the defences were weak. Subsequently, efforts to retake it by surprise attack, blockade and heavy bombardment in the twelfth, thirteenth and fourteenth sieges all failed. These failures were matched by diplomatic defeats, particularly in the early years of the century when Louis XIV sacrificed Gibraltar at Spain's expense to achieve the Treaty of Utrecht. Later all attempts to reverse this were defeated including those following the apparently favourable response of King George I. The century closed with Britain and Spain at war, as Spain was somewhat reluctantly allied with Napoleon at this stage. However, there was soon to be a change in Spanish affiliations and the next century has been aptly described by Dorothy Ellicott in *Our Gibraltar* as 'a century of happy relations with Spain'.

THE BEGINNING OF THE NINETEENTH CENTURY

Under the terms of the Peace of Amiens, signed in 1802, Minorca was returned to Spain; this helped towards establishing more friendly relations between Britain and Spain. In the same year the Duke of Kent, third son of George III, became Governor of Gibraltar in succession to General O'Hara, a colourful character with a distinguished military record. He entertained lavishly and was popular with the garrison and their wives. He was nicknamed 'the Old Cock of the Rock' and was generally well respected, but towards the end of his time discipline had become somewhat lax and there was much drinking of spirituous liquor in the many taverns of the town. The Duke set about correcting this by closing the taverns and establishing a brewery which would provide less intoxicating liquor. The Duke improved relations with Spain by establishing a friendship with General Castanos at San Roque. He was a frequent visitor there to see his mistress, Madam St Laurent, to whom he remained faithful until his royal duties required him to marry to provide an heir to the British throne. This he did in 1819 when Queen Victoria was born. He remained Governor in name until his death in

1820, but was recalled to Britain in 1804 after his attempts to improve discipline had resulted in mutinies by the Fusiliers and the Scottish Borderers; he did not return to Gibraltar.

Gibraltar was closely concerned with Nelson's fleet which visited the port in May 1805 and again after the Battle of Trafalgar in October; this time it brought Nelson's body embalmed in wine before it was sent to Britain. There were other burials of members of Nelson's crews in the Trafalgar Cemetery in Gibraltar, but most of the graves are those of members of the garrison and their families. There had been a serious yellow fever epidemic in 1804 leading to about 1,000 deaths. It has been suggested recently that the epidemic was probably typhus as opposed to yellow fever. The symptoms recorded, however, seem to resemble yellow fever, which could easily have been brought in West African slave ships together with the mosquito responsible, the *Aëdes Aegypti*. These breed quickly in water in small containers probably readily available in the crowded town.

The Battle of Trafalgar removed any threat to Gibraltar from the French fleet. French forces reached San Roque in 1810, but without naval support they would have been unlikely to have much chance of success against the Rock, even if they had attacked. The residents of San Roque must have held this view since some sought refuge on the Rock.

Although it was nearly ten years after Trafalgar before there was an equally decisive land victory in 1815 at Waterloo, from 1811 onwards the French were in gradual retreat from southern Spain. General Castanos was commander in San Roque from the early years of the century and British commanders were always on good personal terms with him. Sir Hew Dalrymple established particularly good relations, which paid dividends when a popular uprising against the French in 1808 brought Spain and Britain into open alliance against France.

COMMERCIAL AND CIVILIAN DEVELOPMENTS

The Napoleonic Wars did not bring sieges to Gibraltar such as it had seen in earlier years, but their effect on Anglo-Spanish relations today was in some ways greater in that a substantial civilian population was developed in Gibraltar. In 1753 the civilian population of Gibraltar numbered 1,816, of whom 434 were British; the remainder were classified as 597 Genoese, 575 Jews, 185 Spaniards and 25 Portuguese. Most of the Jews were from Morocco and connected with trade which had developed with Morocco. Fresh food supplies were imported and British manufactured goods were re-exported. Some of the British civilians were providing services directly connected with the garrison, but other British persons settled in Gibraltar after service in the garrison or as civilians connected with it. They became known as 'Rock Scorpions'.

During the Napoleonic Wars British ships were excluded from some European ports. This led to much greater use of Gibraltar as a port for trans-shipment of cargoes and in turn this resulted in a great increase in civilian population. The population numbered 5,339 in 1801 and more than doubled to reach 11,173 in 1811. After the end of the Napoleonic Wars the population rose steadily to a peak of 17,024 in 1831, although there were some temporary reductions caused by yellow fever epidemics and restrictions on immigration.

An outstanding man in the period between 1814 and 1832 was Sir George Don. He became lieutenant-governor in 1814, but in the absence of the Duke of Kent he was effectively in control from his arrival and remained so until he died in 1832. He gave much attention to civil affairs, as indeed he had to with Gibraltar's severe problems of overcrowding and yellow fever epidemics. This disease had led to the death of over 7,000 persons over a period of ten years, with a further 7,000 having suffered and recovered. Little was known about the mosquito-borne disease, but it was noticed that people who had suffered from it did not get it again.

General Don made arrangements with the local Spanish governor for the settlement of people who had not suffered from yellow fever on the isthmus. This act has later been used as evidence of the lack of British rights over the isthmus. However, a watchtower, known as Devil's Tower, had been built a short distance north of the Rock during the previous century. The isthmus had also been used as a burial ground. Briefly, it can be said that as a matter of courtesy the Spanish authorities were consulted about anything done on the isthmus, which became loosely known as 'neutral ground'.

By the time Sir George Don died in 1832 Gibraltar had become populated by a cosmopolitan people composed primarily of British, Genoese, Jewish, Spanish and Portuguese. There had also been some immigration from Minorca, which developed a population of its own during the eighteenth century before its final return to Spain in 1802. Whilst General Eliott epitomised British defiance in the face of superior odds and caused Spain to suffer a humiliating defeat, General Don was an example of an outstanding British administrator. He solved problems of epidemics and overcrowding by obtaining co-operation from the Spanish authorities across the border. The question of whether Britain had any rights over the isthmus just did not arise. Part of the isthmus became used without any possible consideration of how this might later become a contentious issue. Today the sovereignty of this territory, on which an airfield has now been built, is bitterly argued over.

Similarly there was no contention in General Don's time over the development of a Gibraltarian people. Their identity became an entity partly through George Don's civil administration. Revenue was raised by lotteries, a Supreme Court was established in 1830 and many works were undertaken. Today the Alameda Gardens, the Law Courts, the Exchange Building and St Bernard's Hospital are monuments to George Don's work.

THE SECOND HALF OF THE NINETEENTH CENTURY

In 1848 a very different Governor came to Gibraltar in the person of Sir Robert Gardiner. He was strongly opposed to the style of government set up by Don, and thought Gibraltar should be administered simply as a fortress. He became very unpopular with the Exchange Committee which he described as 'self-constituted and self-elected'. The committee concerned itself with trade in products such as textiles and tobacco; both these items were part of a lucrative smuggling trade with Spain. Gardiner was concerned about the effects of this on relations with the Spanish authorities, but he need not have worried; the trade was profitable on both sides of the border.

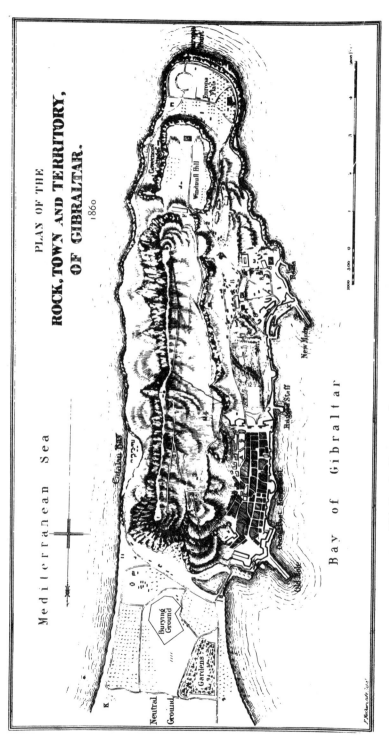

PLAN OF THE
ROCK, TOWN AND TERRITORY,
OF GIBRALTAR.

1860

Mediterranean Sea

Bay of Gibraltar

The Rock, Town and Territory of Gibraltar in 1860

Gardiner's term of office ended in 1855, but he did not go quietly into retirement. He continued to write to Lord Palmerston about the Rock, as he was particularly opposed to the legal system set up by Don. With his trenchant pen he described the Supreme Court as 'an imitative empty pageant of the ceremonies of our high legal courts, full of sound and words, indeed, but of no usefulness in the cases of petty crime peculiar to the place'. His impact on the affairs of Gibraltar was small as the Exchange Committee was well established with powerful contacts in the Lancashire cotton industry and trade both legitimate and clandestine continued. Gibraltarians were indeed becoming a powerful force in their own affairs and showing a will of their own.

The Exchange Committee were undeterred by Sir Robert Gardiner and continued their unofficial activities. In 1873 they wrote to the Secretary of State in London, asking for laws proposed by him or by the Governor for enactment in Gibraltar to be sent to them for perusal. The reply was that this would be 'inconvenient', but a few years later the Exchange Committee achieved success with suggestions put forward for a customs scheme for the port. In the meantime the first statutory body granting powers and duties to Gibraltarians had been set up in the appointment by the Governor, Sir Richard Airey, of Sanitary Commissioners. This followed a cholera epidemic in 1865 in which over 500 people died. The Sanitary Commissioners were active for over 50 years until a City Council was set up in 1921.

The opening of the Suez Canal in 1869 was an important event for Gibraltar, although it did not result in any rapid developments. However, it put Gibraltar on the route to the Far East in the general stream of both commercial and naval traffic. Earlier in the century the use of steamships going directly to their destinations caused Gibraltar to lose some of its importance for the entrepot trade that had grown up during the Napoleonic Wars.

Towards the end of the century a need for a naval base to supplement that established at Malta came into British strategic thinking; this led to the start of building of Gibraltar's naval harbour, begun in 1893. The increasing range of guns after rifled bores started coming into use from 1860 onwards led to the thought that Britain might be better served by possessing Ceuta in North Africa instead of Gibraltar, but nothing came of this. This might have been a popular idea in Spain, but it would have led to much protest from Gibraltarians.

The century ended with war between Spain and the United States, largely conducted around Spanish possessions in the West Indies. The Spanish did, however, begin to reinforce their fortifications around Algeciras, which led to some fears about the safety of Gibraltar. These were not taken very seriously, although one Thomas Bowles MP set to work on an idea that the naval harbour should be built on the eastern side of the Rock to give it protection from shelling from the west. However, he did not make any progress with this proposal.

4
Twentieth-Century Wars

The twentieth century began with work in progress on the naval dockyard, which is a prominent feature of Gibraltar today. It served the Royal Navy well in both world wars and in the period between them. Subsequently, the dockyard and much of the harbour have been turned over to commercial uses, since naval ships are smaller and fewer. Warfare at sea has become transformed since the beginning of the century by submarines, aircraft and guided missiles. At the same time Britain has ceased to be an imperial power with a need for a string of naval bases around the world. Gibraltar still has a part to play as a base for NATO ships in Western Europe, but when the dockyard was built facilities were required for large battleships and the Rock was admirably suited to providing gun platforms for the defence of the base. Warfare based on missiles and the advent of air power have rendered coastal batteries almost obsolete.

There were a number of royal occasions in Gibraltar connected with the building of the dockyard and King Edward VII and Queen Alexandra made separate visits to open dry docks. The royal houses of Britain and Spain came closer together too, with the marriage in 1906 of Princess Victoria Eugenie of Battenburg, grand-daughter of Queen Victoria, to King Alfonso XIII of Spain. The reign was a troubled one which ended in abdication, but with the restoration of the monarchy under King Juan Carlos there have again been signs of closer relations between the royal houses. (There was, however, a set-back when the Spanish King and Queen refused to attend the wedding of the Prince and Princess of Wales, because of the Royal couple's arrangement to board the Royal Yacht in Gibraltar at the beginning of their honeymoon.)

In 1908 the question of sovereignty over the isthmus came to the forefront. For many years it had been customary for British sentries to patrol a line about half-way across the isthmus, but it was decided in 1908 that a fence should be constructed. When the information about the proposal was sent to the Spanish government there was no reply for six months, so work was begun; this led to a protest from the governor of Algeciras. The protest concerned the line of the fence rather than the actual fence and suggested that the line was north of that followed by sentries. This matter was investigated and work continued when it was confirmed that there was no encroachment beyond the limits formerly patrolled.

In April 1909 the Spanish Ambassador in London delivered a note saying that Spain only admitted British territory as being within the walls of the town ceded by the Treaty of Utrecht. There was a British reply in September 1909 stating that there was no intention of departing from arrangements observed by both sides over a long period of time; this remained unanswered. Old maps and a model of Gibraltar made in 1865 (now in the Gibraltar Museum) show that there had been a substantial amount of development on the isthmus half a century earlier. The question remained dormant for another half century, but it was raised again in representations to the United Nations in 1964 and 1965. It has again come to the fore more recently on the question of joint use of Gibraltar airport, which Spain claims is on Spanish territory.

WORLD WAR I

The thirty years following the outbreak of World War I in 1914 were years of great bearing upon Gibraltar, Britain and Spain and on Anglo-Spanish relations. World War I opened quietly for Gibraltar and the Rock was not at the centre of events, as it was later to become. However, World War I presented the British Navy with its first real challenge since the Battle of Trafalgar. The Battle of Jutland far away in the North Sea was comparable with Trafalgar as an action between battle fleets, but the biggest challenge to the Royal Navy came from submarines. Gibraltar had a role in trying to prevent submarines getting into the Mediterranean and out again, but its guns were not of great use in this, as there was little chance of catching a submarine on the surface in daylight. However, the armament of fourteen 9.2-inch guns and eighteen smaller guns formed a formidable defence of the harbour and was particularly useful for convoy collecting and searching neutral shipping for contraband. The 9.2-inch guns had a range of about 15 miles and were still operational in World War II.

There was never any likelihood of Spain becoming hostile, but the Governor of Gibraltar for the war years, General Sir Herbert Miles, had to exercise considerable tact in maintaining good relations with the Governor of Algeciras; he succeeded well in this and also in getting the wholehearted support of Gibraltarians. Just before the end of the war Sir Herbert Miles was succeeded by Sir Horace Smith-Dorrien, who was able to turn his attention to civil affairs in much the same way as Sir George Don had done after the Napoleonic Wars. The Civil Hospital set up a century earlier was extended, and other works were undertaken. More significant for Gibraltarians, however, was the setting up of a City Council with five nominated members and four elected members in 1921. This was a modest beginning in democratic government and gave Smith-Dorrien some direct means of being in touch with Gibraltarian views. The Council took over the duties of the Sanitary Commissioners and provided local government functions on the pattern common in Britain. In 1922 an Executive Council was set up from *ex officio* members and three unofficial members appointed by the Governor; the unofficial member could take part in the debates but could always be out-voted by the *ex officio* members.

It was the invariable practice for governors of Gibraltar to be senior army officers with the rank of General or Lieutenant-General. They naturally regarded their main concern as being the garrison, but some showed a considerable flair for civil matters; Smith-Dorrien set the pattern in this direction. Economic prosperity was based largely on activities in the port, where bunkering and chandlering of ships was the main function. A tourist industry also developed based on cruise liners and a few winter visitors from Britain.

RELATIONS WITH SPAIN

Relations with the Spanish authorities after World War I remained cordial and the dockyard provided work for several thousand Spanish workers who crossed the border each day. The general situation in Spain was one of political turmoil immediately after World War I, but some stability came after a military coup was approved by Alfonso XIII in 1923. Primo de Rivera administered the country until he was succeeded by another army officer six years later. There were elections in 1931 and the Republican Party came to power. Alfonso XIII left the country without formally abdicating, but effectively Spain became a republic without any firm direction. There was violence against the Church and little was done to prevent this. Viewed from Gibraltar the situation in Spain suggested to Gibraltarians, most of whom were Roman Catholics, that they were much better off under British rule. They had perhaps equal dislike for both republican chaos and direct military rule as it had been seen in Spain.

Political events in Spain were a reflection of much of the rest of Europe, which had been severely shaken by the appalling casualties of World War I and the Russian Revolution. Various new forms of politics became common which in Spain went under names such as Marxism, socialism, communism and anarchism. The reaction elsewhere to these politics was the setting up of dictatorships most notably in Italy and then in Germany.

Mussolini, the Italian dictator, led the way towards war with military action against Abyssinia, which became an open war in October 1935. Britain had taken naval precautions in sending ships from the Home Fleet through the Straits of Gibraltar to reinforce the fleet at Malta and in the Eastern Mediterranean. There was sufficient naval strength to deny the use of the Suez Canal to the Italians and stop their operations based on Eritrea and Italian Somaliland. No action was taken however, except to condemn the Italian action. An opportunity to stem the rise of the Italian dictator was thereby lost, with far-reaching consequences for Europe and the rest of the world thereafter. Italian forces had completed the occupation of Abyssinia by the summer of 1936 and the Emperor had fled. In the meantime Britain and France had done little other than propose compromise solutions.

In Gibraltar the Abyssinian war brought about the realisation that the Rock was very vulnerable to air attack, which could have been launched from Italy. Military damage would probably have been slight but devastation could have been caused in an overcrowded town and Gibraltar possessed little in the way of anti-aircraft defence.

THE SPANISH CIVIL WAR

In February 1936 a Popular Front Government was elected in Spain composed of the various socialistic parties including communists and anarchists. This resulted in even greater disorder in the country with more attacks on churches and fights on the streets between extreme right- and left-wing groups. The success of a dictatorship in Italy both at home and overseas had not passed unnoticed by the military in Spain, and General Franco and others were certainly spurred on by nationalistic feeling. In July 1936 Franco led the rising in Morocco, whilst other generals took the lead in a well planned operation in Seville, Algeciras and Madrid. The uprising in Madrid failed owing to the ability of the Popular Front Government to mobilise a militia, which was numerous although not well trained. The war was greatly prolonged after this early failure by the Nationalists, as the insurgent forces became known, to take the capital from outside. Early in the war General Mola boasted that he had four columns advancing on Madrid and a fifth inside the city (thus coining the term 'fifth columnist'), but the capital was not taken until shortly before the end of the war in April 1939.

In the meantime Franco was much more successful in southern Spain and became the undoubted Nationalist leader after Mola was killed in an aircraft crash. Gibraltar was in the centre of the early fighting when Franco's main objective was to get Moroccan troops across the Straits in German transport aircraft. There was fighting in La Linea just across the border, and a front developed to the north of San Roque. Refugees from Spain came into Gibraltar in large numbers, and British naval forces were active in rescuing British subjects who had become trapped in Spain by fighting – including some members of the garrison.

There were some warships of the Spanish navy in the Bay of Gibraltar. The crews of these imprisoned their officers in order to support the Republican side and sought supplies of fuel from Gibraltar; they were refused on the grounds that none could be spared. It also seemed somewhat odd to British officers who went aboard that an admiral was imprisoned below decks. The warships were attacked by aircraft from Morocco and some shrapnel from anti-aircraft fire fell on the Rock. There was a protest which was later courteously answered by the military governor in Algeciras.

After Franco's forces entered Malaga in February 1937 the situation around Gibraltar returned to its previous state, apart from the continued presence of some 2,000 refugees camped on land on the isthmus used as a racecourse. At one time in the early days there were as many as 10,000 refugees, and the presence in Gibraltar of many Spaniards with different political views posed some problems. However, Sir Charles Harrington, the Governor at the time, was successful in his dealings with the administrative problems and in maintaining good relations with the military authorities in Spain. He was helped in this by the resumption of the Calpe Hunt held in Spain; the hunt dated from 1812 when hounds were first kept in San Roque. During General Harrington's governorship his wife had the distinction of being the first lady master – a post she held jointly with the Marques de Marzales.

There was some alarm later in the war when four howitzers were erected in the hills near Algeciras in positions from which they could have bombarded the Rock. The object was to have a field of fire over the Straits which were being used by Spanish Republican warships. The arrival of the guns showed up a weakness in the Rock's defences, as it would have been difficult for the howitzers – well sited in a deep hollow – to have been engaged by the guns of Gibraltar with their flatter trajectory type of fire.

The howitzers were reported in the British press and caused some doubts to be cast over the usefulness of Gibraltar as a

British base. In any event, it was well known in military circles that Spanish neutrality in war was a vital factor. Much more important than the howitzers was the presence of units of the German and Italian armed forces in Spain. Britain and France tried to prevent intervention in the civil war and joined Germany and Italy in a naval patrol designed for this purpose. Germany and Italy, however, used this simply as a cover for their activities in support of Franco, whilst the Russians were giving support on a less effective scale to the Republican side. During the course of the naval patrol some ships were damaged including the British destroyer *Hunter* and the German battleship *Deutschland*; both came into Gibraltar with dead and injured sailors. The *Deutschland* later carried out a retaliatory bombardment of Almeria, as she had suffered damage at the hands of Republican aircraft.

The civil war was used by Germany and Italy to try out the use of their air power, including the bombing of civilians; the raid on Guernica is well known but there were also terrorising raids elsewhere. At the same time of the Munich crisis of September 1938 there were still German and Italian air force units in Spain and this led to urgent consideration of Gibraltar's air defences. These matters were put in hand by General Sir Edmund Ironside when he became Governor in 1938; work was started on building an airstrip on the isthmus and attention was given to anti–aircraft defences and civil defence. A notice over a door in Line Wall Road near the Bristol Hotel still clearly reading 'A R P Shelter' is a reminder of this period. The Munich settlement gave a breathing space to Gibraltar and time for German and Italian air force units to leave Spain when the civil war ended in April 1939.

World War II began with Gibraltar far removed from the fighting fronts. It resumed its World War I role examining ships for contraband and as a convoy collecting centre. Efforts were also made to keep German submarines out of the Mediterranean.

THE ROCK AFTER THE FALL OF FRANCE

The collapse of French resistance to the German army in June 1940 brought the war much closer to Gibraltar. Mussolini played a part in this by substituting opportunism for caution and entering the war on the German side. The most immediate concern was French North Africa coming under the Vichy government, as it did, and what would happen to the French fleet. Gibraltar was used by British naval forces to mount an action against the French fleet at Oran. This caused much bitterness between former allies and persuaded 3,000 French troops who had been evacuated to Gibraltar not to continue in the war. The action also prompted the Vichy French to launch a reprisal air attack on Gibraltar causing damage to buildings and some casualties. Happily Spain was not showing any eagerness to join the war, although Franco expressed support from time to time for his fellow dictators.

The question of Spanish participation came to a head in October 1940, after the German failure to mount an invasion of Britain the previous summer. The Germans then hoped to go through Spain and take control of the Straits of Gibraltar; this would at least have rendered the Rock's defences of little use to Britain. Hitler met Franco at Hendaye on the French border with Spain and asked permission to put his plan into effect. Franco refused, although he described himself as non-belligerent as opposed to neutral thus showing a partiality towards the Rome-Berlin Axis powers. Hitler was angered by this rebuff, but did not proceed to go through Spain without permission. His forces would have been well able to do this, but Spain was not free of danger from guerilla groups, particularly amongst the Basques and Catalans. This was one of Franco's considerations in not agreeing to let the Germans move into Spain. He also knew that his country needed to recover from the civil war.

The question of possibly regaining Gibraltar was not a major factor in Franco's decision. If Hitler won the war recovering Gibraltar might not have been difficult, but Franco was not in any case convinced that Hitler was going to win. If Hitler lost, then any recovery of Gibraltar would have been only temporary. There was also a strong possibility that any move against Gibraltar would have resulted in a British seizure of the Canary Islands. This would have been a diversion for British troops, which Britain could ill afford, but neither German nor Spanish naval forces could have prevented such a move.

Failing to move into the Iberian Peninsula and take command of the Straits of Gibraltar has been classified by historians as one of Hitler's mistakes. At the end of 1940 his forces could have dealt with any guerilla activity in Spain. However, it seems probable that his mind was moving more in the direction of attacking Russia. This may have been another mistake, as Britain was still a powerful force in the west, but the war against Russia was a close-run thing.

Until June 1941 when the attack on Russia was made Gibraltar was liable to be attacked at short notice. German airborne troops were in training in the Jura mountains for an attack under the code name Operation Felix. They had found terrain and rock structure similar to that of Gibraltar in the Jura mountains in eastern France.

The threat to Gibraltar after the fall of France in June 1940 led to the evacuation of the whole civilian population of Gibraltar except for about 4,000 persons required for defence works and essential services. Some 14,000 Gibraltarians were evacuated in ships ill adapted for carrying many women and children. Those who went to Jamaica were the most fortunate in going to a climate similar to their own far removed from the war; they also happened to be amongst the first to return. Some civilians were sent to Casablanca while the fate of French North Africa still hung in the balance, and had the frustrating experience of finding themselves back in the Bay of Gibraltar en route for Britain. Initially they were not allowed ashore to see their families, but this was changed when their departure was delayed. During the course of the war many Gibraltarians suffered from air raids on London, but towards the end of the war they were moved to camps in Northern Ireland, which had been vacated by troops preparing to invade Europe. Here the accommodation was uncomfortable, but many Gibraltarians have memories of a warm-hearted reception in Ulster.

The evacuation of many civilians from Gibraltar was generally accepted as necessary by the people concerned. It led to a feeling of being part of the British war effort and this also applied to the civilians who remained in Gibraltar accepting the same dangers as the garrison. Long separation from their families was a considerable hardship for the members of closely-knit families. All this was viewed as a necessary part of the battle against dictatorship, a political system strongly disliked by Gibraltarians.

At sea, war was waged around Gibraltar until the German surrender in May 1945. Efforts were made to prevent the passage of German submarines through the Straits, but this was a very difficult task. There are opposite currents through the Straits at different depths, and different densities of water dependent upon whether cold Atlantic water is flowing into the Mediterranean, or warmer Mediterranean water flowing in the opposite direction. The Germans were able to make use of this to avoid detection.

Convoys collecting in the Bay of Gibraltar were not immune from attack; they were particularly vulnerable to midget submarines operated by Italians. An Italian ship was moored in Algeciras after suffering damage at sea and remained there for the rest of the war. This was used as a base for midget submarines which attached limpet mines to shipping in the bay. On the high seas around Gibraltar there were also substantial losses of both naval and merchant ships. At the end of 1941 the loss of the *Ark Royal* only 25 miles from Gibraltar was a particularly grievous blow. Escorting convoys to Malta was a major task and in August 1942 Operation Pedestal was particularly costly in naval and merchant vessels. Losses amounted to nine supply ships, an aircraft carrier, two cruisers and a destroyer, but five merchant ships reached Malta including the tanker *Ohio* with vital fuel supplies.

After the United States entered the war, large-scale operations in North Africa became a practical possibility. During the months up to November 1942, when General Eisenhower arrived in Gibraltar, preparations for the landings in North Africa under the code name Operation Torch were pressed forward. Part of the work consisted of extending the runway on the isthmus out into the sea. It was realised both in London and Washington that work was going ahead in an area over which Spain might be sensitive. The use of the Bay of Gibraltar also extended beyond normally accepted territorial limits. There was always a danger of a pre-emptive German strike at Gibraltar with or without Spanish permission, but the Germans were particularly heavily engaged in Russia; the end of 1941 was the time of the retreat from Moscow and in 1942 there came the defeat at Stalingrad. Franco was becoming more sceptical about a German victory and did not go beyond making speeches friendly to the Germans, although he could have made the preparations at Gibraltar impossible.

At the end of 1942 British and American troops were successfully established in French North Africa and Gibraltar had changed from being a threatened outpost and harbour to being a forward base. The building of the runway out into the sea had been a considerable engineering feat accomplished with the use of limestone dug out from the interior of the Rock in the course of constructing an underground system of tunnels. This and other work in Gibraltar required a much larger labour force than that available within Gibraltar itself and at one time 13,000 Spanish workers were crossing from La Linea daily. No attempt was made to prevent this and the Germans must have regarded it as unfriendly help to Britain. On the other hand a large amount of information must have reached the Germans about what was happening in Gibraltar.

As well as providing an airfield for operations against the enemy Gibraltar became an important staging post for transport aircraft. It was used by King George VI when visiting troops in North Africa and sadly in July 1943 by General Sikorski, the Polish Commander, who was killed in an accident on taking off from Gibraltar. This event has led to much controversy, but the hazards of flying around the Rock were well known during the years between the wars. Air currents in the lee of the steeply rising mountain are still a danger to be avoided, although experience gained in the early wartime days has resulted in the hazards becoming well known. The cause of the crash of Sikorski's aircraft was probably human error or mechanical failure, but the early days of using Gibraltar's runway were not without difficulties caused by wind and weather. This is more likely to have been the cause than the theory of sabotage first claimed by the German radio a day after the accident and more recently favoured by some writers.

The role of Gibraltar as a convoy collecting centre and a naval base continued until the German defeat in May 1945. Later in the year the dropping of the first atom bombs on Hiroshima and Nagasaki, which brought the war with Japan to an end, was not without significance for Gibraltar. The great fortress and naval base were now destructible by one aircraft dropping a single bomb. Perhaps the many tunnels built during the war might make survival of individuals underground more possible than in many other places, but even this is doubtful. However, as long as war is not fought with nuclear weapons a role for Gibraltar will remain, and has to be taken into account in all considerations of its future.

5
Franco Stakes A Claim

Spain benefitted from Franco's wise decision to keep out of World War II and thus gained time to recover from its own civil war. Non-belligerent support for Hitler and Mussolini attracted some odium from Britain and others, so there was no question of staking any claim to the Rock for a few years. However, Franco only needed to await his opportunity and he was good at doing that. The granting of independence to India, Pakistan and Ceylon in 1948 set a pattern of decolonisation and there was a rapid increase in political awareness among colonial peoples. The Gold Coast (now Ghana), regarded as a model African colony, suffered serious rioting early in 1948 and claimed self-government, which was achieved eight years later. In the case of the Gold Coast, failure to resettle ex-servicemen rapidly was a particular source of grievance associated with a developing political awareness. For Gibraltarians there were hardships caused by the evacuation and slow repatriation. The hardships were to the forefront immediately after the war, but from a long-term point of view the more important effect of evacuation was the development of a greater sense of being British in sharing in the war effort, and at the same time Gibraltarian in having specific problems.

THE RETURN OF EVACUATED GIBRALTARIANS
After the war moved away from Gibraltar following the North African landings, the thoughts of Gibraltarians naturally turned to becoming re-united with their families. This applied both to the men who had remained in Gibraltar and to families who had been evacuated in 1940 to Britain and elsewhere, when Gibraltar seemed likely to be in the front line of the war; as it happened some of the families felt the more direct effects in the bombing of London.

The return of the first evacuees in April 1944 was followed by demonstrations calling for quicker repatriation. Shortage of shipping and the needs of the war both in Europe and the Far East precluded a rapid return, but Gibraltarians had come to see themselves as having strong claims to consideration and demonstrations continued until the end of 1947, when some Gibraltarians had still not returned home. The demonstrations were in some respects the consolidation of Gibraltar's political awakening. Some years earlier in 1942 a party known as the Association for the Advancement of Civil Rights had been formed under the leadership of Joshua Hassan (now Sir Joshua Hassan GBE, KCMG). At the time he was a young member of the Bar, but in various offices he held from 1945 onwards he became a permanent leader of Gibraltarian opinion. Sir Joshua retired at the end of 1987, but he remains a formidable champion of the democratic rights of the Gibraltarians and an opponent of any major concessions to Spain on the question of sovereignty. Coming from a family established in Gibraltar for many generations he has been well placed to represent Gibraltarians. Early in his career as leader of the AACR he gained the agreement of the British Government to granting a new constitution for the City Council with an elected majority and in 1945 his party won all the seven seats available.

THE GIBRALTAR LEGISLATURE

The first Legislative Council was set up in February 1950. This had an elected majority but executive authority was retained by the Governor. An Executive Council was set up, under the chairmanship of the Governor, composed of four *ex officio* members and four elected members. In 1964 this Council was replaced by a new one named the Gibraltar Council with a majority of elected members. In 1969 another new constitution came into force and this still operates with the Gibraltar House of Assembly as the legislative body. The Assembly consists of fifteen elected members and two *ex officio* members presided over by a Speaker. The *ex officio* members cannot take part in votes of confidence in the government. The Governor has remained the executive authority, but he has a Council of Ministers, who are in charge of Government Departments. The advice of the Council has to be accepted by the Governor on defined domestic matters.

The pattern is similar to that followed in other British colonies in the final stage before independence, but elsewhere this phase has been of much shorter duration. The first government elected under the 1969 constitution was formed by the Integration with Britain Party. In 1972, however, a coalition between the Labour Party and the Association for the Advancement of Civil Rights under Sir Joshua Hassan came to power. Sir Joshua remained Chief Minister under successively elected governments until his retirement in 1987. Elections take place every four years, and the voting age is eighteen. The voting system tends to lead to a division of the house on the basis of eight government seats and seven opposition seats. There is no division into wards and every voter can vote for up to eight candidates.

SPANISH DISMAY

The political changes taking place in Gibraltar in the years after World War II were viewed with some dismay from Spain. Progress towards self-government by Gibraltarians was quickly seen as an obstacle to recovery of sovereignty by Spain. A constructive reaction might have been to show friendliness towards Gibraltarians, but instead a contemptuous attitude prevailed, particularly in the press. The withdrawal of ambassadors from Spain by United Nations member countries immediately after World War II made British views less easily available in Spain. Deference to Russia over attitudes towards Spain prevented magnanimity by Britain after the war ended, and gestures of goodwill were only grudgingly given when a Russian threat to peace became obvious through events such as the blockade of Berlin. Franco had kept out of the war, doing little to aid the Germans and Italians to whom he was in fact indebted. Public ostracism of Spain in the post-war era tended to strengthen rather than weaken Franco's position. In 1950 Franco took the opportunity in a Spanish press interview to say that Gibraltar was part of Spain and must be returned, pointing out that governments, whether republican or monarchal, had said this for centuries. Soon after Franco's statement anti-British demonstrations took place, led by Madrid University students. This made the re-establishment of diplomatic relations between Britain and Spain even more difficult, but this was eventually achieved in 1951. Whilst diplomatic relations had been in abeyance, however, Franco had found a theme to stir popular Spanish support.

After diplomatic relations were resumed Spain attempted to begin talks about Gibraltar at ambassador level, but to no avail. In the meantime the Spanish press produced vilification against Britain and generally denigrated Gibraltarians. The situation came to a head in 1954 after a visit to Gibraltar by Queen Elizabeth II and the Duke of Edinburgh, which was represented as an incursion upon Spanish territory. There was a Spanish protest and the Spanish consul in Gibraltar was withdrawn. Some restrictions were imposed on Spanish workers crossing the frontier and no new passes were given. At the time there were over 12,000 workers crossing daily. The restrictions had limited immediate effect, however, due to the lack of work in La Linea, in contrast to Gibraltar where much post-war construction work was in progress as well as more traditional work in the port and dock-yard.

In the years between 1954 and 1963 various diplomatic exchanges took place between Britain and Spain. On the British side the objective was to obtain a lessening of restrictions at the frontier. Co-operation to prevent smuggling was offered by Britain, since smuggling was one reason given by Spain for the restrictions and delays at the frontier; in fact much of the smuggling, which had been customary for generations, was carried out by sea through fishing villages around the coast. On the Spanish side there was also a fear that the airport at Gibraltar might become a main route for entry for British tourists into the Costa del Sol to the detriment of Spanish airports. Britain was pressing for the removal of restrictions at La Linea, but Spain was avoiding talking by imposing a condition that the question of sovereignty must be discussed. Until 1964, however, restrictions at La Linea were an irritant rather than a major issue. There were still nearly 10,000 Spanish labourers crossing the border daily. This was important to Spain as well as to Gibraltar, since there was little work in La Linea, and work in Gibraltar was probably

supporting around 40,000 people in that town, taking depend-
ants into account.

THE UNITED NATIONS TAKE A HAND

An opportunity for Spain in its long ambition to gain recovery
of Gibraltar came through the setting up of a United Nations
Special Committee on Decolonisation. Britain was required by
various resolutions to report to this committee on places under
colonial rule, which included Gibraltar. With a record of granting
independence to colonies when this status was sought, Britain
seemed to have little to fear from a reference of Gibraltar to this
Committee. It was thought that questions were best answered
by Gibraltarians themselves, so it was arranged for Sir Joshua
Hassan and Mr Peter Isola, who were on opposite sides in the
Gibraltar elected legislature, to appear before the committee in
September 1963. They both indicated that they were not seek-
ing independence and were contented in their association with
Britain, colonial though it was.

Spain took the whole exercise more seriously than Britain
and claimed that Gibraltar was not a colony in the same sense
as Malta, Cyprus or other places on the list of dependent territories. It was rather a piece of the Spanish mainland; this had
been colonised and thus Spain was a victim of British colonial
expansion. In putting forward her case Spain might have been in
difficulty over her own enclaves of Ceuta and Melilla in North
Africa, but these territories had been incorporated into mainland
Spain; thus they did not have to be reported to the UN as
colonies. Otherwise, the situation would have been found to be
almost identical, as the territories had been acquired by conquest
from former Sultans and subsequently recognised by treaty.

The debate before the Special Committee was adjourned and
resumed in September 1964 just after the revised constitution of
1964 for Gibraltar had been put into effect. This had made another move towards democratic government by Gibraltarians in
abolishing the Executive Council and replacing it with a Gibraltar
Council composed of five elected members of the Legislative
Council and four *ex officio* members appointed by the Governor. The Special Committee however, failed to see the new

constitution as a further indication that Gibraltarian representations were given freely and without any undue influence from Britain. The Committee was used to representations demanding self-government and was apparently confused by the people of a small territory not wanting to break away from a colonial power. A resolution was passed calling on Britain and Spain to find a negotiated solution taking into account the opinions expressed by members of the Special Committee and bearing in mind the interests of the population of the territory. The Committee referred to paragraph 6 of Resolution 1514 (XV) which reads:

6. Any attempt aimed at the partial or total disruption of the national unity and the territorial integrity of a country is incompatible with the purposes and principles of the Charter of the United Nations.

The Committee did not refer to paragraph 2, which reads:

2. All peoples have the right to self-determination; by virtue of that right they freely determine their political status and freely pursue their economic, social and cultural development.

The two paragraphs are in direct conflict when applied to Gibraltar. The Committee applied one of the paragraphs and simply referred to the interests of Gibraltarians without according them rights to determine their future. The Gibraltarian representatives suggested that paragraph 6 was not intended for their situation but to protect colonies from neighbouring predator states. They indicated that they wanted free association with Britain as their form of self-determination, but the Committee was adamant that the territory should be returned to Spain and was apparently satisfied by Spanish promises regarding the interests of Gibraltarians. The idea that there should be self-determination by Gibraltarians in respect of their interests was disregarded.

SPANISH SENSE OF VICTORY

Spain had achieved a great success before the Committee on Decolonisation. This had been done by much hard work in preparing and presenting their case. They had the advantage of support from South American countries with strong Spanish ties, such as Venezuela and Uruguay; Britain on the other hand was left with little support apart from that from Australia. The Spanish success was remarkable in that after World War II Spain had been virtually ostracised, and even seven years later there was still a reluctance amongst some member countries towards Spanish admission to the UN. By 1964, however, the same body had come to treat a Fascist dictatorship as a colonised country and was suggesting that reluctant Gibraltarians should join it. Within Spain Franco had seized upon a popular issue to gain support and become less dependent for his power upon the Army, the Falangists and the Church.

Britain had handled the affair with too much expectation that democratically elected representatives from Gibraltar would be accorded a right to self-determination. There had also been a lack of forthrightness by Britain in dealings with Spain in trying to suggest that constitutional changes in Gibraltar were for administrative convenience only. Spain was claiming that the Rock was being alienated to the Gibraltarians in breach of the Treaty of Utrecht. The short answer at that stage could have been that whatever changes were being made in the constitution of Gibraltar, Her Majesty Queen Elizabeth II was remaining sovereign and there was no question of offering sovereignty back to Spain.

Several courses of action were open to Spain after the favourable UN resolution. One line of approach would have been to adopt a conciliatory attitude towards Gibraltarians. Instead, steps were taken to make their life more difficult. Within a few days of the passing of the UN resolution on 17 October 1964, the Spanish authorities at La Linea adopted measures to make crossing the frontier more difficult and long queues of cars developed. The reason given for the delays was the prevention of smuggling; this had suddenly become most important. The British view was that the restrictions amounted to duress and that there could be no negotiations until the situation at the frontier was restored to normal.

In March 1965 Spain admitted for the first time that measures of a harassing nature were being taken; the measures were said to be the result of British failure to negotiate. Only Spanish workers were to have passes to cross the frontier to go to work in Gibraltar and passports issued by the Government of Gibraltar were no longer recognised. As a result Gibraltarians who at the time lived in Spain and worked in Gibraltar had to move over the border. This exacerbated an already difficult housing situation and Spain also took the further step of banning the export of building materials to Gibraltar.

Restriction imposed by Spain were deliberately designed to have an immediate adverse effect on Gibraltarians and the Gibraltar economy without increasing unemployment in La Linea. Consequently, the number of Spanish workers crossing the border only reduced gradually and time was gained for setting up development works around La Linea including an oil refinery near the ancient Roman settlement at Carteia.

In Britain possible retaliatory measures were considered, but rejected because of the inevitable repercussions on Britain's own economy. One action was taken against Spain, however, although not intended to be connected with the dispute. This was a refusal to build frigates for Spain in Britain, initiated by the Labour Government which came to power in 1964 as a gesture against a dictatorship; it damaged British industry as well as being an irritant to Spain.

SPANISH RED BOOKS

In 1965 a Spanish Red Book on Gibraltar was published. This was a long and well prepared work from the point of view of stating the Spanish case. It alleged British breaches of the Treaty of Utrecht, including the contention that Britain had encroached on the isthmus, and sought to deny the right of Gibraltarians to be considered as a people; they were stated to be simply a population in a fortress.

In December 1965 the UN General Assembly called upon Britain and Spain to hold talks. These began in London in May 1966 with a Spanish request for a recision of the Treaty of Utrecht. In return an agreement was offered on British use of Gibraltar as a military and naval base, and Gibraltarians were to be given a special status within Spain. They would be allowed to continue under their own civil laws, while freedom of speech and religion were to be guaranteed. A town council was to be set up which would become the tax raising body. It was hardly surprising that these proposals had little appeal to Gibraltarians who had seen their interests so flagrantly injured by Spanish measures at the frontier. Britain continued to put forward the view that the wishes of the Gibraltarians were paramount, so no progress was made towards a solution. Spain for her part continued throughout 1966 to apply increasing measures against Gibraltar. In January military flights from NATO countries were stopped from flying over Spain. In August female workers were stopped from crossing the frontier with the intention of causing as much damage as possible to the hotel industry in Gibraltar, and in October the frontier gates were closed to vehicles.

The years 1963–69 were rich in the publication of papers and resolutions, but these were the source of controversy rather than agreement. A second Spanish Red Book was produced in 1968 and there were a number of British White Papers between 1965 and 1968. The complete closing of the frontier did not come until June 1969. The labour force crossing the frontier regularly had by that time become reduced to 4,666. The Algeciras–Gibraltar ferry was closed later in the month and on 1 October telephone and telegraph services were cut. Thus Spain had brought about the isolation of Gibraltar and its people whilst demanding the handing over of sovereignty by Britain.

THE REFERENDUM

In December 1966 a resolution was passed by the Fourth Committee of the UN calling on Britain to expedite, in consultation with Spain, the decolonisation of Gibraltar. This committee had the 1964 report of the Special Committee before it, and Britain voted in favour of the resolution as it referred specifically to the interests of the people of Gibraltar. Accordingly Britain arranged a referendum which was held in September 1967.

The people of Gibraltar were asked to say which of the following alternative courses would best serve their interests:

A.   To pass under Spanish sovereignty in accordance with the terms proposed by the Spanish Government to Her Majesty's Government on 18 May 1966.

B.   Voluntarily to retain their link with Britain with democratic local institutions and with Britain retaining its present responsibilities.

A team of observers from the Commonwealth unanimously reported that the referendum gave a free expression of choice through a secret ballot. The result was 44 votes for A and 12,138 votes for B.

There could hardly have been a more convincing result regarding the wishes of the people of Gibraltar. It must, however, be said that the terms offered by Spain were far from clear to the voters. A Spanish appeal to the voters giving a brief description of the offer could have been made, but Spain preferred to condemn the referendum. Support was given to this attitude by the Fourth Committee of the UN in December 1967 when Britain was invited again to decolonise Gibraltar in accordance with paragraph 6 of Resolution 1514 (XV); paragraph 2 referring to self-determination was once again ignored. This attitude was difficult for British people to understand. Since the end of World War II self-determination for the inhabitants of colonies had become a pillar of British policy. Ballot boxes had been taken to remote places on the African continent and elsewhere to give the people a chance to vote for representatives, who in turn became the government of the country. When the elected government requested independence it had invariably been granted. These governments did not necessarily continue with democratic ways and some became more authoritarian than Spain was under Franco. There had, however, been a choice and Britain could not possibly deny this to Gibraltarians whatever the United Nations might resolve. In December 1968 there was a General Assembly Resolution calling on Britain to decolonise

Gibraltar not later than 1 October 1969 in accordance with previous resolutions. This meant handing Gibraltar over to Spain. Britain, however, continued with its own plans for granting a greater degree of independence to Gibraltarians by setting up the Gibraltar House of Assembly.

Recovering Gibraltar had taken on the nature of a crusade in Spain. There was little economic or strategic value from a Spanish point of view, but the issue had come to the forefront as a nationalistic one. Spain had been skilful in getting support in the UN by means of presenting Britain as an imperialistic coloniser of Spanish territory. This had been done over 250 years previously through the Treaty of Utrecht, but Spain now introduced the question of the airport being on territory not unequivocally ceded by the Treaty. This became an excuse to make the use of air space around Gibraltar more difficult, and was a means of presenting Britain as a usurper of land which was still Spanish. Britain suggested that the disputed points in the Treaty of Utrecht should be submitted to the International Court of Justice at The Hague, but Spain refused to do this. Spain's case was by no means indisputable and there was little point in risking a defeat at The Hague when they had so clearly won the ear of the UN.

THE ISTHMUS

The natural isthmus between the Rock and the mainland is a sandy strip about ten feet above sea level. It is now almost entirely covered by the airport runway, buildings, concrete and tarmac. For many years the term neutral territory was used to cover the whole area including that beyond the border fence erected in 1908. After the fence was erected the tendency was to refer to the part on the Spanish side of the border as neutral territory; the Spanish customs post and other buildings were a few hundred yards beyond the British fence and the intervening land was left in its sandy undeveloped state.

In the Red Books on Gibraltar a big issue has been made out of the alleged British encroachment and the dispute over sovereignty. There are two Spanish claims. First, there is the claim to the whole of Gibraltar by virtue of UN policy on decolonisation.

Second, there is the claim that the territory of the isthmus north of the town and its old fortifications has never been ceded. The first claim, in Britain's view is completely answered by the rights of Gibraltarians to self-determination also enshrined in the United Nations Charter for all peoples. The second claim is met by the old custom of jurisdiction over land within a cannon-ball shot of a fortress and the use of land on the isthmus for over one-and-a-half centuries. There have only rarely been Spanish objections until recent years. The objections to the fence erected in 1908 was originally made against the line taken by it, which the governor of Algeciras alleged was north of the line patrolled for many years by British sentries. This matter was amicably resolved between the local authorities concerned, but there was a Spanish protest through their ambassador in 1909 stating that only the town and fortress were ceded by the Treaty of Utrecht. The British reply to this based on custom and usage was unanswered and there the matter rested for half a century. This included the period of World War II when Spanish workers were freely employed on work connected with the development of the airfield.

Spain has complained about British breaches of the Treaty of Utrecht, but the biggest breaches came in 1727 and 1779, when Spain laid siege to the Rock. On both occasions the isthmus was used as a base for attack, thus representing the reasonableness of exercising jurisdiction up to 1,000 yards beyond a fortress. The problem of the isthmus should be a small one, but it can be made a big issue at almost any time. In 1987 an EEC agreement over air fares was blocked for a time by Spain on the grounds that it could not countenance the inclusion of Gibraltar as a British airport – a question considered in more detail later.

THE YEARS AFTER 1969

The final closure of the frontier in 1969 to pedestrians as well as to vehicles was felt mainly in the loss of Spanish workers, but Gibraltar had already begun adapting to a closed frontier. Workers from Morocco had begun to replace those from Spain, and more were found after the Spanish workers were completely cut off in 1969. Arrangements were made for some Moroccans to come over on a weekly basis and return by air or sea to

Tangier at weekends. Others took up residence in Gibraltar. The construction industry was badly affected in the earliest days of the closed frontier, and having to provide housing for Moroccans was an added difficulty in a place already short of accommodation. Nearly all building materials including sand had to be imported by sea.

The need to bring imports of everything used in Gibraltar from Morocco, Portugal, Britain or elsewhere and the loss of some tourist trade had an adverse financial effect on Gibraltar. Britain provided around £2 million per annum in development aid in the years following the frontier closure and construction work on housing and other buildings continued with reasonably little disruption. The tourist industry had been partly based on visits from Spain of one or two days until the frontier was closed to vehicles in 1966; in 1964 there was a total of 738,000 visitors to Gibraltar. A few visitors continued to come from Spain until the Algeciras ferry was closed in June 1969, but the pattern had to change if the industry was to survive. The Gibraltar Tourist Office set to work on this with considerable energy and developed with tour operators visits of one or two weeks. Encouragement was also given to cruise lines to continue calling and bring money into the Main Street shops.

Gibraltar was at a disadvantage compared with the Costa del Sol in Spain through having few bathing beaches, but the ones available were developed and this was also applied to other tourist attractions such as St Michael's Cave and the old defences of the Rock. A pattern developed of between 30,000 and 40,000 tourists visiting Gibraltar for an average time of about a week. Package holidays which included Morocco also became available so that visitors to Gibraltar did not suffer from the isolation caused by the closed frontier. The situation was quite different for permanent residents, who could only leave by sea or air for Tangier or by air for Britain instead of being able to walk across the frontier. Economically there was not much hardship, as the functions of the port in supplying fuel oil and other needs to ships continued and work went on as usual in the naval dockyard. The Main Street shops suffered most from the loss of visitors from Spain on shopping expeditions, but this had run down after the 1966 closure of the frontier to traffic.

The most cruel blow was to people with relatives in La Linea. The only route to visit them was via Tangier and Algeciras making a costly journey of about 100 miles. It became a common practice on Sunday afternoons for families to go out to the frontier and shout the latest news across the frontier to the Spanish families who were kept by Spanish barriers about 100 yards distant. Field glasses were also used to get a better view of the latest born member of the family.

The Spanish actions, far from making Gibraltarians want to surrender to their wishes, brought about an attitude of defiance and some contempt. There was a small Spanish naval vessel which patrolled from time to time along a line which Spain claimed as territorial waters and this became known locally as *Smokey Joe*. It left clouds of black smoke in its wake and there was an apocryphal story that it was burning cork waste from the Andalusian cork woods.

There was relatively little diplomatic activity between Britain and Spain during these latter days of the Franco regime. The matter again came before the Fourth Committee of the UN at the end of 1974, but without any changes of attitude. The few people in Gibraltar who did advocate some concessions to Spain, tended to keep quiet, mindful of a noisy demonstration in 1968 which followed the publication of a letter in the *Gibraltar Chronicle* signed by persons calling themselves 'The Doves', which suggested some kind of bargain with Spain.

On the Spanish side activities designed to gain support from the world at large for a return of Gibraltar were continued. There were no further Red Books, but a book published in Britain in 1974, *Rock of Contention* by George Hills, gave further weight to the Spanish case. It was based on a detailed historical study going back to Moorish times, but the recent history placed the accent on the UN demand for decolonisation. It was a valuable work in that it put forward the Spanish case in a way that it had never been done in Britain. The book did not give much weight to the main British point that the Gibraltarians are a people with a right to self-determination. It

65

is perhaps difficult to disagree entirely with the last sentence of *Rock of Contention*:

> The cynic could well conclude that nothing had changed in seven centuries of the history of Gibraltar – it remained the outstanding example of the unreasonableness of men with nothing to warrant the hope that men would reason in the future, or if they did, allow reason to prevail.

It is fair to add that perhaps some men have been more unreasonable than others, and it is hard to see unreasonableness in the Gibraltarian wish for self-determination.

6
Gibraltar After Franco

Franco's death in November 1975 was an event of great moment in Spain. It was nearly forty years since he had started the nationalist uprising in Morocco and later assumed supreme power in Spain. Before he died he made provision for a reversion to a monarchy after his death nominating Juan Carlos, grandson of Alfonso XIII, as king. Thus far a course had been set, but Franco probably did not expect a rapid move towards a democratic form of government to be made so soon. This change towards democratic government fully occupied Spanish leaders immediately after Franco's death and matters affecting Gibraltar fell into the background; thus an opportunity to show immediate goodwill towards the Gibraltarians was lost. An opening of the frontier to pedestrians from both Gibraltar and Spain would have removed hardship and given hope. As it happened even telecommunications were left closed until Christmas 1976 and then only opened for a short period. After elections in Spain in June 1977 the next gesture was another re-opening of telecommunications for the following Christmas; on this occasion the opening was said to be temporary, but the lines were in fact left open.

In Gibraltar in the meantime there was little inclination to make any moves towards gaining Spanish friendship, and candidates in the election of 1976 who favoured early talks on relations with Spain attracted few votes. Sir Joshua Hassan's party won a majority with the rest of the Assembly being divided between Independents and the Gibraltar Democratic Movement led by Mr Joe Bossano.

In November 1977 and in March 1978 meetings were held in Strasbourg and Paris respectively between the British Foreign Secretary Dr David Owen and the Spanish Foreign Minister Señor Oreja. The Chief Minister Sir Joshua Hassan and the

Leader of the Opposition Mr Maurice Xiberras were present as part of the British delegation and participated in the discussions. This was the first time that the elected government of Gibraltar was given some sort of recognition. These meetings led to nothing more than a setting up of study groups and it became clear that any Spanish recognition of the rights of Gibraltarians to self-determination would only come about very slowly. It would in any event have been difficult for a Spanish government relying on votes of the electorate in Spain to change course on Gibraltar against the nationalistic fervour built up during Franco's long period of office. On the British side there remained the unequivocal commitment in the Gibraltar Constitution of 1969 not to give up Gibraltar against the wishes of the people.

THE LISBON AGREEMENT

In May 1979 a Conservative government was elected in Britain and there was a meeting between the new Foreign Secretary, Lord Carrington, and Señor Oreja in New York in September. This led to a more formal meeting in Lisbon in April 1980 when a document was signed which became known as the Lisbon Agreement. This document left details of matters such as the opening of the frontier to be worked out, but it was hoped that there would be an early opening at La Linea. Much time was subsequently spent on working out details and there were differing views on priorities. The British view was that the first step was to open the frontier, but Spain thought all subjects should be discussed together. The issue of sovereignty, moreover, kept hindering progress.

The year 1981 was beset with complications for Spain and for Anglo-Spanish relations. In February there was an attempt in Madrid by Lt-Colonel Tejero to lead a military take-over of the Spanish Parliament and in July relations with Britain became soured over the Prince of Wales and his bride joining the Royal Yacht *Brittania* in Gibraltar to start their honeymoon. The arrangements had earlier led to King Juan Carlos and Queen Sofia cancelling their attendance at the royal wedding. The year passed without any progress towards the opening of the frontier.

A move might have been made during the first half of 1982, but the war over the Falkland Islands intervened in April. Gibraltar was used by naval ships going to the South Atlantic and work was done in the dockyard to fit out the cruise liner *Uganda* as a hospital ship. There was considerable sympathy in Spain for the Argentinian claim to *Las Malvinas* as the islands are known in Argentina; the situation was seen in Spain as similar to that of Gibraltar. There are important differences, and the subject will be examined in a later chapter together with the settlement over Hong Kong and the existence of the Spanish overseas territories of Ceuta and Melilla. No two cases can be precisely the same, but similarities lead to generalisations which are sometimes misleading..

In June 1982 Spain made a formal request to postpone action on the Lisbon Agreement and nothing happened until December, when there was a limited opening of the frontier for persons crossing on foot; this applied only to Gibraltar residents or Spanish passport holders. Consequently the opening was not of any value to the Gibraltar tourist industry, but it was appreciated by families on both sides of the border who had suffered from a closed frontier for over thirteen years. A socialist government was elected in Spain in October 1982 and a meeting between Señor Fernando Moran, the new Spanish Foreign Minister, and Mr Francis Pym, who had succeeded Lord Carrington, was held in March 1983. Further progress on the Lisbon Agreement was prevented by Spanish insistence on dealing with the sovereignty question whilst the British attitude was that first the frontier must be fully opened. Economically, limited opening was working to the Spanish advantage, as locally produced food and other items were freely bought in Spain whilst the Spanish Customs were very strict in ensuring that Spaniards did not take any purchases into Spain from Gibraltar. In the meantime a more serious threat to Gibraltar's economy was arising from the British Government's decision to close the naval dockyard and to maintain only a relatively small naval base. The dockyard was to be handed over to private enterprise, but it was clear that without considerable initial help a commercial dockyard could not become viable. In July 1983 negotiations between the British and Gibraltar governments led to a British undertaking to grant aid of £28 million to meet conversion costs and to provide naval work for three years from 1985 onwards.

Relations between Britain and Spain suffered a set-back soon after the meeting between Señor Moran and Mr Pym. In April 1983 a visit of British naval vessels to Gibraltar was the subject of a Spanish protest. For over a century it had been customary for Spring exercises to take place around Gibraltar; Spanish protests had been common during the latter years of Franco's government, but they had ceased after the Lisbon Agreement. In April 1983 some of the ships were those which had taken part in the Falklands war, including *HMS Invincible*. The precise reasons for the Spanish furore over an annual event were not quite clear, but there was still a strong feeling of sympathy for Argentina in their claim to *Las Malvinas* and perhaps the inclusion of ships such as *HMS Invincible* causd Señor Moran to order the protest, although the customary information had been passed in advance to the Spanish Ministry of Defence. Two Spanish frigates and a destroyer were sent from Cadiz to watch from the waters around Algeciras. When the fleet left, the Spanish destroyer *Langara* watched from a distance of about one mile for the purpose described by Spanish naval officers as 'emphasising Spain's presence in waters of its national jurisdiction'. By chance the destroyer bore the same name as the admiral captured by the British fleet in 1780 and rowed ashore by Midshipman Prince William (later King William IV). By another historical chance Prince Andrew was aboard *HMS Invincible*.

It had become common practice for Gibraltar to be used by ships from other NATO navies as well as ships of the Royal Navy, and Britain would have welcomed some co-operation with the Spanish navy within a NATO command. In 1983, however, the Socialist government of Señor Gonzalvez, elected in 1982, was committed to a referendum on Spanish membership of NATO. Although there was later a favourable vote, Spain remained outside the NATO command structure. This did not, therefore, provide any way forward.

In most respects Anglo-Spanish relations were good after the introduction of democracy in Spain; it was only over Gibraltar that they tended to be in disarray through the Spanish insistence on sovereignty. Many other questions concerning Gibraltar were considered in a constructive manner and the prospect of progress came in connection with Spain's request for accession to the European Economic Community (EEC). Spain applied to join the community in 1977, but negotiations proceeded very slowly. France and Italy voiced fears of adverse agricultural competition and there were problems within the EEC itself over the budget and the Common Agricultural Policy, which had become a very costly item. Britain had less to fear from Spanish agricultural competition than Italy or France and generally welcomed the prospect of Spanish accession. Thus there was a point of common ground between the two countries, but Britain adopted the line that Spanish membership of the EEC without a fully open frontier with Gibraltar was inconceivable.

Spain was still trying in 1983 to combine the question of sovereignty over Gibraltar with progress on a complete opening of the frontier. However, as the prospective date for joining the community, 1 January 1986, came closer there was a realisation that the frontier would have to be fully opened. There were meetings at various international conferences between ministers on both sides, but it was not until the end of 1984 that the whole business was seriously tackled.

THE BRUSSELS AGREEMENT

At a meeting in Brussels between the British Foreign Secretary Sir Geoffrey Howe and the Spanish Foreign Minister Señor Fernando Moran, on the 27 November 1984, agreement was reached that the frontier would be completely opened to traffic and all persons before the 15 February 1985. The British government for its part agreed to discuss the issue of sovereignty, although the commitment to honour the wishes of the people of Gibraltar as set out in the Constitution of 1969 was firmly stated. It was agreed that the general principles of the EEC would apply to all citizens of Spain and Gibraltar subject to a transitional period related to Spain's joining the EEC. During such a period it was agreed that preference would be given to citizens of either side when granting work permits for Gibraltar. Spain undertook to make improved provisions for air safety around the Rock, and working groups were to be set up to deal with co-operation in economic, cultural, touristic, aviation, military and environmental matters.

In opening the frontier Spain was implementing measures which would have been required later on joining the EEC. On the British side there was the concession that sovereignty could be discussed along with other matters. This was hailed as a diplomatic triumph in Spain. Señor Moran described it as 'the biggest diplomatic success for Spain over the Rock since 1713' and other commentators were saying it was the first time since 1713 that Britain had agreed to discuss sovereignty; King George's 'promise' of 1721 was temporarily forgotten.

In Gibraltar the agreement was generally welcomed. It was seen as of great economic value and Sir Joshua Hassan stressed that the sovereignty question was still subject to their wishes. The position on sovereignty had not changed as far as they were concerned.

The gates at the frontier were opened to traffic on 5 February 1985. There were fears in Gibraltar about the effect of the opening on employment. Gibraltar was virtually free of unemployment whereas there was a different situation in La Linea, so granting rights to Spaniards in Gibraltar caused some apprehension, particularly with the prospect of less work in the dockyard. However, there was immediately a substantial gain for Main Street shops and for business in general. The tourist industry profited immediately through tour operators being able to function freely on both sides of the frontier and through coach trips into Gibraltar on a daily basis. Banks also benefitted, since the scope for business with British residents on the Costa del Sol and with tourists was widened.

In general administrative arrangements made at local level worked well, but the question of use of the airport by travellers from or to Spain proved a difficult problem. The matter came to a head when Spain blocked an EEC agreement on air fares in June 1987 on the grounds that the inclusion of Gibraltar as a British airport could not be countenanced. The old arguments about the land on the isthmus not having been ceded by the

Treaty of Utrecht were raised once again. The matter became the subject of negotiation in London in December 1987 between Sir Geoffrey Howe and Señor Francisco Ordonez, the Spanish Foreign Minister in succession to Señor Moran. An agreement was reached, under which the inclusion of Gibraltar Airport as an EEC airport for purposes of the Air Fares Agreement was made subject to the Gibraltar Government agreeing to passengers to and from Spain not having to pass through Gibraltar customs and immigration controls. In the absence of such agreement Gibraltar Airport would remain outside the EEC agreement on air fares. Other points agreed upon by the foreign ministers concerned reducing delays at the frontier, a re-opening of the Algeciras ferry and the setting up of a committee to co-ordinate the work of the Gibraltar air terminal and a new terminal to be built on the Spanish side of the frontier. It was firmly stated that both Britain and Spain reserved their respective positions on sovereignty and that this issue was not affected. In Gibraltar there was a general welcome for the British attitude of leaving the issue for the Gibraltar Government to decide, but a reluctance amongst politicians to commit themselves on the matter with an election to be held within a few months. Sir Joshua Hassan, who had taken part in the negotiations with his deputy Mr Canepa, chose the moment to announce his retirement from the office of Chief Minister. This had been expected before the next election in accordance with his previously expressed intentions. As far as the agreement was concerned Sir Joshua refrained from expressing a personal opinion, but said he would not use his majority in the Assembly to gain its acceptance.

The timing of Sir Joshua's retirement was difficult. He could not leave the task of reaching agreement over the airport to his deputy, but he also needed to give Mr Adolfo Canepa some time in office before the election a few months ahead. When the election came in March 1988 the GLP/AACR government of Mr Canepa was defeated by Mr Joe Bossano's Gibraltar Socialist Labour Party (GSLP). This party has a strong trade union base and its leader played a prominent part when trade unions were at the zenith of their power between 1974 and 1978. At the end of the period parity in wages with those in the United Kingdom was agreed and brought relative industrial peace. The Gibraltar Transport and General Workers Union in which Mr Bossano held office played a substantial part in achieving parity of wages.

There were a number of socialistic policies in the election campaign of the GSLP including an emphasis on spending money on housing programmes, but much of the appeal to voters came from outright opposition to the Brussels Agreement and the later accord between Britain and Spain over the airport. The GSLP pledged itself not to take further part in negotiations stemming from the Brussels Agreement. The Agreement had been a step forward in that it resulted in the opening of the Spanish frontier, but British agreement to negotiate on sovereignty caused some fears in spite of frequent assertions by British Ministers that nothing would be ceded without the approval of the Gibraltarians. In effect Britain's undertaking to negotiate goes no further than agreeing to consider Spanish sovereignty over Gibraltar if it is wanted by Gibraltarians.

In the election of 1988 the GSLP obtained over half the votes cast and the remainder went mostly to the GLP/AACR, but about ten per cent were taken by the Independent Party led by Mr Joe Pitaluga, a well respected retired civil servant who entered the contest shortly before the date of the election was announced. The GSLP obtained eight out of fifteen seats in the Assembly, the other seven being won by the GLP/AACR. Mr Pitaluga's party was thus left without a member of the Assembly. He died a few months after the election and this tragedy has left the future of his party in doubt.

The adoption of a strong bargaining position by Spain in claiming sovereignty over the airport led to fears amongst Gibraltarians who voted for the GSLP; these were not allayed by Spain's ultimate readiness to agree to quite a simple arrangement whereby travellers to Spain could land at Gibraltar and go straight to a Spanish customs and immigration building. The GSLP has now ceased sending a Gibraltar Minister to take part in Anglo-Spanish discussions on Gibraltar, so it is doubtful whether any progress regarding the airport can be made for some time.

The GSLP government has given much attention to achieving viability for the dockyard as a commercial shipyard. After being a naval dockyard for most of the present century it now has to become competitive with other shipyards. The outlook for repairing small boats is much better and the government has set up a joint venture with private industry for this purpose. For the dockyard itself a new sense of purpose amongst the labour force can probably help more than anything towards future prosperity. The naval dockyard was often at the centre of industrial disputes, so some changes in attitudes have become necessary. A comparison with Gibraltar's commercial port shows how an enterprise based on ocean transport can establish a reputation for efficiency and be profitable. The shipyard needs to build up something similar to play its part in Gibraltar's future prosperity based on open sea, land and air communications.

PROGRESS SINCE THE LISBON AGREEMENT

The period immediately following the Lisbon Agreement in 1980 was one of stagnation caused by Spanish insistence on the sovereignty issue coming up for discussion at the same time as other matters, and British insistence that first the frontier must be opened. Since then there have been set-backs but on the whole steady progress has been made towards a better understanding on both sides. Spain is now a member of EEC and apart from disagreements over Gibraltar relations between Britain and Spain have been friendly. Spain has shown both a greater willingness to regard the Gibraltarians as having rights and a better understanding of the British commitment to the Gibraltarians. Both foreign ministers concerned in negotiations with Britain in recent years, Señor Moran and Señor Ordonez, have said that they do not want the Gibraltarians, but they want the Rock. It is undoubtedly something symbolic that they want, but sovereignty over the Rock and over the people who live there are seemingly indivisible. There have been Spanish suggestions of a lease-back arrangement whereby the territory would be ceded to Spain, but leased back to Britain for a period, or a condominium with some form of joint sovereignty. Neither arrangement would be satisfactory from a Gibraltarian point of view, although the possibility of a condominium arrangement leaving the Gibraltarians free to run their own

75

affairs seems worthy of a long-term study. During his visit to Britain in April 1986 King Juan Carlos hinted that perhaps the royal houses of Britain and Spain might play some part in resolving the one obstacle to completely cordial relations between the two countries.

On the plane of practical matters affecting Gibraltar much progress has been made, and local co-operation on health, safety and crime prevention has been good. In May 1985 Gibraltar services were made available to help deal with a serious tanker fire alongside the oil refinery wharf near La Linea and in March 1988 there was very effective co-operation over an attempt by the IRA to plant a bomb in a car in Gibraltar. In the latter case there was close co-operation both between British and Spanish governments and between the police forces on each side of the frontier. The three persons who parked a Spanish-registered car in Gibraltar, apparently to reserve a parking space, were shot and killed in Gibraltar. They had parked another car in La Linea and later a car containing a bomb was found parked in Marbella. The IRA had a well-devised plan, foiled only through the co-operation of Spanish police.

From a Gibraltarian point of view time is needed to allay the fears engendered by Spanish imposition of a closed frontier and Spanish contempt of their rights as a people. The Spanish view that they are merely a population within a fortress and not a people has been less in evidence in recent years. There is, however, a fear on the part of Gibraltarians of what they describe as becoming absorbed into Spain by a kind of 'osmosis'. Thus a loosening of immigration and customs controls at the frontier causes Gibraltarians some alarm. It might perhaps cause less alarm if seen as part of a general process of absorption in Europe as frontiers lose their importance. For the present Gibraltarians still feel a need to assert the right to be considered as a people to which their history entitles them.

7
Gibraltarians and Their Culture

When the case of Gibraltar was before the UN in 1963 and subsequent years the Spanish Red Books sought to show that the Gibraltarians were a population living in a fortress, rather than a people with rights to self-determination. Such rights have been framed by the UN and other bodies in somewhat loose terms and confusion arises when, as in the case of Gibraltar, territory has been ceded at some time to a colonial power. There is a direct conflict between Spain's demand for the return of territory and the wish of Gibraltarians to determine their own future. Their claim to be a distinctive entity is based upon settlement on the Rock over a long period of time since the British and Dutch landed in 1704. It is a claim similar in nature to the undisputed one of Trinidadians or Mauritians, for example, to be considered as a people. There has in the case of Gibraltar been a similar settlement of a mixed people over a long period of time.

SETTLEMENT ON THE ROCK

The settlement of Genoese, Moroccan Jews, Spanish, Portuguese and British persons in Gibraltar during the first half of the eighteenth century has already been mentioned. The effect of the Napoleonic Wars has also been outlined, but the process of settlement in Gibraltar has been a continuous one up to present times. During the Napoleonic Wars there was a widening range of immigrants and as well as Spanish, British and Genoese, there were Italians (non-Genoese), Minorcans, Maltese, French and Sicilians. At this time the classification of people by nationalities became slowly obscured in reports on population. There was, however, a tendency for settlers on the Rock to group themselves together in certain areas according to nationality. For instance, the Spanish and Portuguese tended to live in the Cooperage

District at the end of Main Street near the Waterport whilst the British tended to live around King's Bastion.

Classification of population by trades in the period of rapid growth during the Napoleonic Wars is significant. The trades sections of the registers distinguished between natives and other nationalities showing a process of assimilation of a Gibraltarian people. Minorcans were prominent amongst persons engaged in trades and the inclusion of Minorcans as a category is worthy of note in that they were themselves a mixed people. Minorca had changed hands between Britain and France during the seventeenth century before finally being ceded to Spain in 1802; the immigrants to Gibraltar from Minorca were largely of French and British stock and well attuned to garrison life. Amongst trades cigar making assumed a considerable importance based on trade with Spain, mostly illicit smuggling. By 1834 there were 540 persons employed in a cottage type industry making cigars. The actual smugglers were a floating community but they formed a distinctive group; in 1834 one person even dared to register as a resident smuggler.

Catalan Bay on the eastern side of the Rock is an interesting settlement in that it started as a summer fishing camp for Genoese fishermen, who returned home in winter. This continued into the nineteenth century, but by 1814 there was some more permanent settlement and the population included Spanish and Portuguese persons. The separateness of Catalan Bay has continued into present times and there is a tendency for marriages to take place within the community. Fishing no longer provides the livelihood for the village, which has become more occupied with catering for the tourist industry based upon the Caleta Palace Hotel and the bathing beach in the bay. The separateness of Catalan Bay is apparent in the custom there of referring to the town of Gibraltar as being around the other side. It has, however, been usual for a long time for Catalan Bay residents to work around the other side, and the dockyard has been a source of skilled employment for some residents for most of the present century.

The whole process of assimilation of the population of Gibraltar into a distinctive people has been a gradual one over a period of about 275 years. Throughout these years British and

Spanish elements have become merged into the population, but at certain periods there has been immigration by other distinctive groups, such as the Genoese in the eighteenth century. The Maltese came later and were particularly prominent after 1873, when the Aliens Order in Council restricted free entry to 'British' persons, who included those from Malta and elsewhere in the British Empire. At this time the Maltese were not particularly popular; amongst their occupations was that of goatherd and their goats tended to wander.

The origins of Gibraltarian names are worth some study, although today these do not necessarily represent a person's ancestry with any degree of accuracy. There has been much inter-marriage over the years since, for example, the first Genoese Bassadone or Baglietto came to the Rock. The Jewish community has been fairly cohesive as it is elsewhere in the world and Hebrew names such as Hassan, Levy and Serfaty are fairly common. Members of the Jewish community are prominent in business and the professions and some adhere very strongly to their religion. Happily Gibraltar has at almost all times been a place of great tolerance towards Jewish people. Other groups such as the Maltese are much less distinguishable but Maltese names include Cassar, Mifsud and Zammit. Garcia is a Spanish name well known on both sides of the Spanish frontier and there are many Gibraltarians with English and Scottish names, although perhaps not so many as one might expect of those common in Britain, such as Brown or Smith. Marriage between British persons working in Gibraltar and Gibraltarians or Spaniards has been a source of assimilation of population in recent times as well as in earlier generations.

CENSUS REPORTS

The method of compiling census reports has changed over the years, but the system used at present has been little changed since the Census of the Population Ordinance was passed in 1868. From 1871 until 1931 inclusive members of the British forces and their families were excluded. Over that period the population remained fairly steady. It was 18,695 in 1871, rose to 20,355 in 1901 and fell to 17,405 in 1931. There was no census in 1941 owing to the war, and the next census was in 1951. This census included families of members of the forces, but not the servicemen themselves, and the total population enumerated was 20,845. Later census figures produced in 1961, 1970 and 1981 have distinguished between Gibraltarians, British (other than Gibraltarians and families of British servicemen), Non-British, Families of Servicemen, Visitors and Transients. The most important figure is that for Gibraltarians for whom Gibraltar is their home. In 1961 the figure was 17,985. It rose to 18,873 in 1970, when some 800 Gibraltarians formerly resident across the border in Spain had returned following the imposition of restrictions on movement across the border. The figure in 1981 was 19,825, so in round figures it is correct to say there are about 20,000 Gibraltarians, who are resident in Gibraltar and for whom it is their home. There are of course other Gibraltarians resident and working overseas who are none the less interested in the future of their homeland to which they return from time to time.

On census night in 1981 the total number of persons present in Gibraltar, excluding servicemen but including their families, was 29,616 so it can be said again in round figures that about 30,000 people live on the Rock. Amongst other persons enumerated on census night in 1981 families of servicemen numbered 2,265 and other British persons numbered 3,706. The total for non-British persons was 2,923 of whom 2,040 were Moroccans. Amongst the remaining non-British persons there were 217 persons of Asian origin who are largely engaged upon trade in Main Street shops. They form a fairly cohesive group of their own and whilst not Gibraltarian they have a considerable interest in Gibraltar's future.

There have not been any great changes in population since the census of 1981 which was taken when the frontier was closed. A few Gibraltarians have, however, moved to live across the frontier where housing is more readily available and less expensive. It is now once again possible to cross the frontier daily to get to work and some Spanish workers also do this. The census of 1970 was held a year earlier than normal in order to assess the changes brought about by the closing of the frontier, but then as now there was no great effect on total population. Gibraltarians had returned, Spaniards had left and Moroccans had come. Changes in composition of population after the opening of the frontier in 1985 seem to have been happening only slowly.

GIBRALTARIAN CULTURE

Gibraltarians had more social and cultural affinity with Spain early in the century than they have today. There were easy trading and family relationships across the border and Gibraltar's Main Street shops and markets had a more Spanish flavour. The bars in Main Street were Spanish in style and British sailors were able to enjoy Spanish entertainment when in port. Others freely crossed the border to visit Gibraltar Street in La Linea where young ladies were not under stringent colonial laws governing entertainment.

The decline in contact started through a turning away from Spain during the period leading up to World War II owing to instability and civil war in Spain. During World War II Gibraltarians were closely associated with Britain either on the Rock itself or as evacuees to Britain. They felt themselves similarly opposed to dictators. Later there came thirteen years of a closed frontier to turn their affinity further away from Spain and towards Britain. Gibraltarians also developed their own cultural activities and it happened that difficulties on the Spanish frontier almost coincided with the opening of the John Mackintosh Hall in 1964.

John Mackintosh, a Scot born in 1865, was a successful businessman engaged in shipping enterprises in both the City of London and Gibraltar. He was married to a Gibraltarian and set up a company in Gibraltar. He died in 1940 leaving a trust fund for the purpose of encouraging interest in British culture in Gibraltar. During his time the Spanish language was used in Gibraltar much more than English in commercial and social life and the Spanish influence was strong as it still is in art and music. John Mackintosh Hall has helped to give both British and Spanish cultural influences a particularly Gibraltarian flavour. The hall provides a meeting place for many clubs and societies with interests including drama, photography, stamp collecting and chess.

There are rooms for exhibitions of art, photography and similar activities and there is also a gymnasium. The building caters within its walls for many recreations and interests which could be found in an English town of similar size. Although Gibraltar is a small place it is hardly surprising that with its varied sources of ancestry it has become a distinctive centre on its own.

The diversity of Gibraltarian culture is apparent in its religious life. The Roman Catholic faith predominates and the census figure of 1981 for Roman Catholics was 19,747; next comes the Church of England with 2,259 followed closely by Muslims who are mostly Moroccans with 2,124. The Jewish faith had 589 adherents and smaller numbers are listed under various other Christian churches. The Cathedral of St Mary the Crowned in Main Street is the centre of the Roman Catholic Church, but there are a number of other churches – mostly of nineteenth-century design – both inside and outside the town area. An interesting church outside the town is St Teresa's, which is a monument to both faith and ingenuity, as it was constructed out of old Nissen huts on the edge of the airport. It had become needed in this area to serve the housing estates built nearby after World War II. The parish priest for many years was one Father Devlin, who in November 1984 found himself unexpectedly translated to become the Bishop of Gibraltar after the sudden death of the holder of that office.

During earlier centuries there has been much more religious toleration in Gibraltar than in either Britain or Spain. One British Governor, General Bland, according to notes for his successor written in 1751, thought that Protestants should be encouraged to settle on the Rock and there were signs of some concern at other times over the predominance of Roman Catholics, but in general relations with that church were good. The Anglican Cathedral of the Holy Trinity was built in the time of Sir George Don and he was buried in it when he died in 1832.

The British colonial influence has been strong in matters such as education as well as in government. The pattern of mission schools common in British colonies was initiated in 1831 by S. H. Rule, a Methodist minister. Big steps forward were made when Dr Scandella became Roman Catholic Vicar Apostolic in 1855 and from his time onwards there was steady development along similar lines to Britain. A Minister of Education is responsible to the Chief Minister for educational matters, and there are eleven primary and middle schools catering for boys and girls up to the age of twelve years and a boys' comprehensive school and a girls' comprehensive school for older children. Gibraltar also has a technical college, but university and other higher education takes place in Britain or elsewhere outside Gibraltar.

A British pattern in Gibraltar's institutions is also to be found in trade unions. There is a Trades Council on the TUC pattern and the strongest union is the Transport and General Workers Union, which has close links with the British union of that name. It has recently been active in opposition to the disposal of the naval dockyard to a private consortium. Mr Joe Bossano, leader of the Gibraltar Socialist Labour Party (GSLP) elected to form the Government in 1988, has also been a prominent officer in union affairs.

The health service likewise has close British links. The service is mainly based upon St Bernard's Hospital with over 180 beds and the King George V Psychiatric Unit, but schools have a special service of their own. Visits are sometimes made to Gibraltar by British specialists and there are arrangements under which hospitals in Britain take patients who cannot receive all the treatment required in Gibraltar. Since the frontier was opened co-operation has been developed between Gibraltar and Spain in health matters. There was a fear that the Gibraltar service might become overloaded with work arising from Spanish people visiting and working in Gibraltar, but this has not happened.

THE SYSTEM OF GOVERNMENT

Religion and language would pose only minor difficulties in respect of the integration of Gibraltar with Spain. The problems in respect of institutions, law and government, however, would be at the other end of the scale. An outline has already been given of Gibraltar's constitution, which gives the Rock a high degree of independence. The offer in 1966 by Spain to set up a town council which would raise its own taxes would have been a very poor substitute for the degree of independence Gibraltar already enjoyed, particularly as it came from a dictatorship regime. Spain's return to democracy has made a difference, but there is still a great lack of trust resulting from the years of frontier restrictions and closure.

There was at one time a party known as the Integration with Britain Party; this was led by Mr Peliza and formed the first government under the 1969 constitution. However Britain stated that neither total integration with Britain nor even some kind of Channel Islands-style status of dependency would be acceptable. Action along these lines would have put any possible future agreement with Spain out of the question and would have caused constitutional problems both for Britain and Gibraltar. The constitution of 1969 is well adapted to a move to Dominion status or independence, having been used elsewhere in a similar form. The Governor still retains ultimate executive authority with defence, external affairs and internal security remaining reserved subjects, but domestic affairs are within the control of ministers. The Governor is required to act in accordance with the advice of the Council of Ministers on domestic matters, although there are certain reserve powers of disallowance (not used in practice). The capability of Gibraltar to run its own affairs under a Governor-General can hardly be in doubt after the long period of successful working of the current constitution. However, this system would be impracticable without the agreement of Spain, and that cannot be forthcoming as long as there is insistence on sovereignty.

The Spanish government has shown a willingness for Gibraltar to operate with its own laws and with a high degree of independence within Spain, but there would be substantial difficulties in any such arrangement. Having separate laws might sound reasonable and in some respects similar to the distinction within Britain between English and Scottish law, but the practice would be far more difficult.

GIBRALTAR'S LEGAL SYSTEM

The mark of British legal systems has been firmly on Gibraltar since the middle of the eighteenth century. Spanish law applied before 1704 and probably continued to do so after the British arrival for civil matters, personal rights and relationships. Military tribunals dealt with criminal matters for the civil population as well as the military, and the Prince of Hesse appointed Alonso de la Capella as judge in 1705. The first Charter of Justice came in 1720, under which a judge named John Beaver was appointed to preside over a court of summary jurisdiction for personal suits. The Charter was granted by George I and it is interesting that the law applicable was to be that of Spain, particularly as at about the same time he was in communication with Philip V of Spain regarding the restoration of Gibraltar to Spain. As far as the local population were concerned the provision is a curious one as there were few civilians of Spanish nationality in Gibraltar at the time. There are no details available of the composition of the population, but there were certainly some Genoese who may have been there before 1704 and lived under Spanish law.

A second charter was granted by George II in 1740. It was not promulgated in Gibraltar, but was held to be applicable by the Privy Council. The charter contained the unequivocal words: 'We will that the laws of England be the measure of justice between the parties.' It is uncertain whether the charter marked a change of attitude and a determination to make the Rock British following its successful defence in 1727, or whether it simply took account of what was happening. Judges appointed in Gibraltar would have been familiar with English or Scottish law and would have tended to be guided by these principles, even though the earlier charter said that Spanish law was to be applied.

Criminal jurisdiction seems to have continued to be by military tribunals until another charter set up justices of the peace on the British model in 1752. There were no further substantial changes until 1817 when the population of Gibraltar had grown substantially as a result of the Napoleonic Wars. Then a fourth charter revoking previous charters set up a Small Debts Court, a Court of Civil Pleas, a Court of General Sessions (with almost unlimited criminal jurisdiction), a Court of Quarter Sessions, the Assize of Bread (concerned with quality and price) and a Court of Appeal. The population at the time was about 12,000, so Gibraltar was somewhat excessively endowed with courts and there was also a proliferation of judicial officers; these included a judge advocate who as the governor's representative could sit on any court at any time.

The system was rationalised in 1830 by a fifth Charter of Justice under which the judge advocate disappeared and was replaced by a judge heading the newly constituted Supreme Court. The holder of this office became known as the Chief Justice in 1841, when Sir James Cochrane held the post in which he remained until 1877. There has been a continuous process of development of the legal system in Gibraltar from the fifth charter down to the present time. The Constitution Order of 1969 set out the current position under which there is a Court of Appeal, the Supreme Court, the Court of First Instance and the Magistrate's Court. The last two of these correspond respectively to county courts and magistrates' courts in England. A stipendiary magistrate normally presides over the Magistrate's Court, but two justices can sit in his absence. The Supreme Court exercises jurisdiction similar to that of the High Court and the Crown Courts in England. Criminal trials on committal from the Magistrate's Court are conducted by the Chief Justice sitting with a jury. Appeals from the Magistrate's Court and the Court of First Instance go to the Supreme Court, and thereafter there are rights of appeal to the Court of Appeal and the Judicial Committee of Privy Council in London. The Gibraltar Court of Appeal is constituted by visiting justices from Britain and other Commonwealth countries.

Admiralty jurisdiction in Gibraltar is now vested in the Supreme Court, but it is a very old jurisdiction having begun with a Vice-Admiral's Court established in 1739. This played an important part in dealing with prize cases affecting captured ships and cargoes during the Napoleonic Wars. In 1872 it heard the well known case of the *Mary Celeste* found abandoned at sea near the Straits of Gibraltar. What happened has never been satisfactorily established; the sails were set and the ship was in good order with plenty of food and water on board, but the ship was completely deserted.

The law to be applied in Gibraltar was defined in 1740 as the law of England in 1740, but the present position stems from an Order in Council of 1884, which applied English law as it existed on 31 December 1883. A Gibraltar ordinance passed in 1962 applies English common law and equity from time to time in force to Gibraltar and specifies certain United Kingdom Acts as applicable in Gibraltar. Most statute law is, however, based on ordinances passed in Gibraltar. The application of Gibraltar statutes within the Spanish kingdom might not pose insuperable difficulties, but the whole system of English law, particularly common law and equity, is so different from that of Spain that problems could be expected. The common law and equity in England are not static, but are constantly being adapted by judges to contemporary circumstances. The law of negligence is a case in point. This has in recent years been greatly affected by successful actions being fought for negligent statements as opposed to negligent acts. The building surveyor who says that weak foundations are sound may find himself just as liable to damages as the driver who causes an accident by not putting on his hand-brake. It is doubtful whether developments of this nature could be applied in a different kingdom.

Trial by jury is another facet of English law which differs greatly from the inquisitorial system applied in continental countries. Under the continental system, an enquiry by a judicial officer is followed by a trial by a judge, whereas the adversarial system of English law involves a prosecution and a defence being put before a judge and jury; the judge guides the jury on the law, but the jury have to decide in a criminal trial whether or not the prosecution has proved its case beyond reasonable doubt. The differences between the two systems are less marked in the case of summary trial by magistrates, but in civil law affecting private rights, duties and relationships the continental systems were greatly influenced by the reception of Roman law in the fourteenth, fifteenth and sixteenth centuries. In England, common law and equity developed as a progression of judge-made law over many centuries, and the process still continues. There is also much statute law affecting civil relationships, but this is nothing like the Civil Code found in continental countries. In Spain there are some local variations, as in the case of Catalan law, but great difficulty would arise in having different basic legal concepts in different parts of one kingdom. Countries with strong common law influences tend to place emphasis on what is reasonable and how the ordinary man or woman would see a problem. A learned judge many years ago used the colourful phrase 'the man in the Clapham omnibus'. When confronted with such a phrase, a judge in Madrid could well ask where is Clapham and what has the man in the omnibus to do with the case?

The legal problems described are illustrative of cultural differences between Gibraltarians and Spaniards brought about by different histories. The problems may not be of overwhelming importance in themselves, but they would assume large proportions if Gibraltarians were unwillingly forced to join Spain. The closed frontier has accentuated differences in turning Gibraltarians more towards Britain and away from Spain. From the beginning of January 1983 Gibraltarians have had the right to register as British citizens under the British Nationality Acts. Some, when registering in that year, found to their surprise that they had no need to register as they were already British citizens through having been born in Britain during the years of World War II.

The right to register as British citizens was greatly welcomed, but the height of fervour for being British came during the years of the closed frontier. Subsequently there has been a rise of feeling of being Gibraltarian with rights within Europe. This was evident in a visit to Strasbourg in September 1987 by Sir Joshua Hassan as Chief Minister and Mr Joe Bossano as leader of the opposition. The visit was strongly opposed by Spanish MEPs and was of symbolic rather than of practical value. It created difficulties for Lord Plumb as the British President of the European Parliament, who was accused of insulting the Gibraltar delegation by asking them to his residence instead of his parliamentary office. From a Gibraltarian point of view, the visit was a move towards gaining acceptance as a small state in its own right, but Lord Plumb clearly wished to avoid giving any recognition to this.

THE GIBRALTARIAN ROLE IN NATO

Since World War II Gibraltarians have come to play a substantial part in their own defence which is integrated into NATO. There is an active naval unit named *HMS Calpe*, a shore-based establishment with an operational role concerned mainly with communications. The unit was formed in 1965 and was named after a World War II destroyer. She was the second *HMS Calpe*; the first was a re-named Spanish sloop captured in 1800.

The Royal Naval Reserve Unit in Gibraltar is the only such unit existing outside the United Kingdom. It is composed of part-time volunteers on the same basis as units in the United Kingdom and undertakes the same type of training in conjunction with the Royal Navy. It has expanded steadily since its formation and does not have difficulty in attracting volunteers.

The Army is likewise represented by a unit known as the Gibraltar Regiment. This has some full-time members as well as part-time volunteers. The Regiment is a gunnery unit and mans the old 9.2-inch guns still left on the Rock as well as smaller and more modern artillery weapons. Both the naval and the army units provide guards of honour for ceremonial occasions and the gunners fire salutes.

If Spain should become completely integrated into NATO commands, there would be a chance of developing co-operation with the Gibraltarian components of NATO. However Gibraltarians would no doubt view such co-operation with some misgivings at first, and gestures of friendship from Spain would be needed to show clearly that the Gibraltarian units were to be accepted on a basis of equality. With their knowledge of Spanish, Gibraltarians could provide a useful liaison role between British and Spanish forces. An even greater advantage of closer co-operation would be bringing together of young Spanish and Gibraltarian people. Such links have been lacking as a result of the years of the closed frontier and need rebuilding.

Successive Spanish governments have moved a long way from the attitudes of General Franco, but the closure of the frontier has had the effect amongst other things of turning the younger generation away from Spain and Spanish culture. Interest in visiting Spain is greater amongst those who used to go there before the frontier restrictions than amongst the younger generation who have grown up with a closed frontier. Their economic future must, however, necessarily be greatly affected by free trade and free movement across the border. Gibraltar's prosperity is inextricably bound up with this as it has been for most of its history.

8
Commerce and Industry

From the earliest British days in Gibraltar, commerce and civilian activities have been based on supplying goods and services to the garrison and operating the port facilities. Over the years the port has built up and adapted its services to the needs of the time. The Napoleonic Wars were a period of expansion when British ships were excluded from many other ports. There was a decline in the years following these hostilities and the arrival of the first steamship, the *Royal George*, in 1823 did not augur well for Gibraltar; steamships tended to go direct to their destinations instead of using the entrepot facilities of the port. The opening of the Suez Canal in 1869 was better news for Gibraltar, which benefitted from a steady increase in the use of the sea route to the Far East through the canal. An ocean liner route from Britain grew up which reached its peak in the years between the world wars. Then ocean liners heading for India, the Far East and Australia called on a regular basis on their outward and return journeys. The port was also used by liners from Italy on trans-Atlantic routes. During this period pleasure cruising in liners taken off their normal routes developed, and this has now become the only form of ocean passenger travel through the port.

THE PORT AND THE BALANCE OF TRADE
The long history of Gibraltar as a port has resulted in its gaining a reputation for efficient services to ships. Oil, food and water are supplied and medical services are readily available. The medical services are particularly useful for British ships and for British seamen on foreign ships due to the lack of language problems and the facility of communication with hospitals in the United Kingdom if necessary.

Figures for shipping tonnage entering a port can be confusing since different systems of measurement exist but in terms of gross registered tonnage on average between 20 and 25 million tons enter the port each year. The number of ships varies between 1,200 and 1,900. Whilst the tonnage is greater than it was in the years between the world wars, the number of ships is much less owing to the general increase in the size of ships. The port facilities have been greatly improved through the use of the naval harbour, which between the world wars was only used by Royal Navy ships and troop ships. Now most ocean-going ships and tourist liners can load and off-load alongside the North Mole, or at jetties in this area.

Imports into Gibraltar exceed £100 million in value, but exports are valued at less than £50 million. Fuel oil for ships accounts for about one-third of the imports and three-quarters of the exports. Nearly all the other exports are also re-exports, as Gibraltar has virtually no agriculture or production industry of its own. A balance of trade is largely brought about by tourism, banking and other services. The most marked increase in recent years has been in banking services. Attention was turned in this direction when the frontier was closed and from 1970 onwards there was a steady increase in deposits. These were made both by individuals and by companies registering offices in Gibraltar but not trading in Gibraltar, thus obtaining substantial tax concessions. In 1970 deposits in banks amounted to around £10 million, but by 1986 the figure had increased to £300 million. Inflation accounts for some of this increase but nothing like the thirty-fold one that has taken place. The opening of the frontier has been of great benefit to banks, since they can now provide a useful facility for the many British residents in southern Spain; this has contributed towards an increasing rate of growth. British and international banks are well represented and recently Spanish banks have opened branches in Gibraltar.

THE DOCKYARD

Since the beginning of the century the dockyard has been a source of employment for Gibraltarians and Spaniards. In recent years Moroccans have replaced Spaniards, but there has been a tendency for Gibraltarians to be more in evidence in the skilled trades, so the British Government's decision to close the naval dockyard and hand it over to private ownership was viewed with dismay in

Gibraltar. It was, however, a decision in line with action on dock-yards of older standing such as Chatham and Devonport in the United Kingdom. There was some postponement in Gibraltar's case, but the yard was closed as a naval dockyard at the end of 1984, shortly before the frontier was fully opened. Some £28 million of aid was given by the British Government to help the yard achieve viability under a company known as Gibrepair, in which the Gibraltar Government was the only shareholder. The management of the yard was put in the hands of A. & P. Appledore, a British company based in Devonshire, but there were frequent disagreements between them and the board of Gibrepair. There was also a considerable amount of industrial unrest between the management and the yard's 800 employees. Disputes arose over wages, but an underlying fear of job losses was the major problem. There was some guaranteed naval work, but this was only on a temporary basis. As the naval base continues in existence there may be some work to be done on naval ships from time to time, but work on major refits will only be available in competition on a commercial basis. The arrangement with A. & P. Appledore was terminated in 1988 by the GSLP Government and the Deputy Chief Minister took over the management of the yard.

The main problem over the shipyard is common to all EEC shipyards in a lack of work to utilise the resources available; competition from Japan, Korea and Taiwan has had a great effect although these countries are far away. The previous Gibraltar Government tried investing to 'salvage the yard' but the EEC has ruled that such action is against a directive on shipyards. Before ship repairing was brought in under Gibrepair a small shipyard situated to the north of the airport runway was in operation; this has now been closed, but there are two yacht marinas to the south of the runway. Providing services and doing repairs to small ships and yachts is being developed and, apart from employment in the dockyard, there are some 1,500 persons employed in other marine engineering and repairing work.

BUILDING CONSTRUCTION AND OTHER INDUSTRY
The building of new housing and the improvement of other buildings suitable for modernisation began soon after World War

II. Since 1948 around 4,000 new dwellings have been provided and the construction industry presently employs about 2,000 persons out of Gibraltar's total workforce of around 12,000. The industry has been supported by development grants from the British Government, but has also been substantially financed by the Gibraltar Government and by private sources. Apart from housing there has been much commercial building and re-building in recent years. The industry has always been handicapped by its need to import most of the materials required. Sand is now obtained from the eastern side of the Rock, but at one time all building requirements were being imported.

Only about six per cent of Gibraltar's housing stocks of around 8,000 dwellings are owner-occupied. About three quarters of the remainder are rented from the government whilst the rest are privately rented. The government always has a long waiting list for accommodation, but the GSLP Government is making strenuous efforts to tackle the housing shortage. Housing is mostly in blocks of flats which is inevitable in the confined space available on the Rock, but the social problems of high-rise flats in Britain seem to have been largely avoided.

The building of hotels and other facilities for tourists has also been a feature of the construction industry since World War II. Most of the new building took place before the frontier was closed in 1969, but there is always some extension and rebuilding work in progress.

There is a little light industry in Gibraltar which depends to some extent on the tourist trade, but in the main all of Gibraltar's needs are imported as finished products. There are bottling plants for beer and mineral waters, but once again much is imported ready for sale. An enterprising light industry call Gibrocks has been set up behind a shop in Main Street in which items made from stalagmite are sold. The material is collected from scrap obtained in tunnelling operations and processed through a tumbler into small smooth pebbles. A polish is then applied and the pieces of rock thus produced are fitted into pieces of jewellery. Larger pieces of rock are used in paper weights and other *objets d'art*. Certificates are given stating that the stones are genuine pieces of the Rock of Gibraltar.

There is probably more scope for local processing of items for purchase by tourists.

THE TOURIST INDUSTRY

The financial value of the tourist industry to Gibraltar cannot be accurately assessed as it is made up of so many sources of income. The hotels are the main beneficiaries from visitors who stay in Gibraltar, but there are also many day visitors from Spain who spend money in the Main Street shops and elsewhere.

During the sixteen years of a closed frontier nearly all visitors arrived by air from Britian; a few also came across from Tangier by air or by sea on the cross-Channel steamer *Mons Calpe* which was in operation at the time. Such arrivals in most years numbered between 40,000 and 50,000 persons. These have increased to over 100,000 since the frontier has been open and over two million have arrived annually by land from Spain since the frontier opened fully in 1985. Some of the visitors from Spain stay for a few days in Gibraltar, but the majority are on day visits; many come in coaches or in cars, which has created traffic and parking problems. Visitors from cruise liners have generally been between 70,000 and 90,000, bringing trade for both shopkeepers and the operators of sightseeing tours around the Rock.

Throughout the period of the closed frontier the airport was Gibraltar's lifeline. Various Spanish restrictions on its use were imposed relating to Spanish territorial waters and the crossing of the Spanish mainland, but they all stopped short of making the airport impossible to operate. With so many possibilities of retaliation against Spanish airlines, this would have been unwise. Now Gibraltar airport itself provides a useful landing point for visitors to places such as Sotogrande at the southern and developing end of the Costa del Sol. There are, however, difficulties over customs and immigration, which have already been mentioned. In most instances it is probably preferable for travellers to take the shorter road journey to their Spanish destination in spite of having two sets of immigration and customs controls. Co-operation at local level between officials on both sides of the border is generally good-humoured and the difficulties of two sets of immigration and customs need not cause too much trouble.

Gibraltar has a variety of hotels, suiting different tastes and offering a fairly wide price range. The Bristol and the Montarik are two of the older hotels situated in the town. The former building, in Cathedral Square, dates back in part to 1865. The hotel was opened in 1890 and has belonged to and been managed by the Piccone family ever since. During the first part of the century it catered mainly for families of naval officers and for members of the garrison. It has been modernised extensively since World War II; this has been an almost continuous process until the present day. It now provides the visitor with a central position in a comparatively quiet part of the town and there is a pleasant garden on the opposite side of Bomb House Lane which runs into Cathedral Square along one side of the hotel. It can be expected to appeal to people who like old hostelries in British towns.

The Montarik, situated at the north end of Main Street, is partly composed of buildings which formed part of the Grand Hotel, which was of similar style to the Bristol in the years before World War II. Like the Bristol the Montarik provides a convenient situation in the town. At the southern end of the town the Queen's Hotel stands just outside Southport Gates on bus routes near the Alameda Gardens. The most modern hotel within the town is the Holiday Inn, which is comparable to establishments of the same name elsewhere. It stands in Governor's Parade and was opened in 1973. There is a marked contrast between the hotel and the Garrison Library opposite it together with the older buildings in the square which forms Governor's Parade. The effect is not as unpleasing as might be expected and the hotel itself provides excellent views of both the Rock and the bay from its higher floors; there is a swimming pool at the top of the building.

The Rock Hotel was a product of the period between the two world wars. When it opened about six years before World War II it was outstanding as a Gibraltar hotel. Situated about 500 yards outside the walls of the town up a steep slope, on the road to Europa, the hotel commands excellent views across the Alameda Gardens to the harbour, the bay and the hills west of Algeciras. The interior has a spacious elegance reflecting the period during which it was built; lounge suits are now the

Europe Point and Lighthouse. (*G.T.O.*)

(*Overleaf*) The Rock from the south. (*By courtesy of the Royal Navy. Photograph by L/Airman (Phot) C. North.*)

View to the north-west into Spain from the Upper Rock, showing the cable car. (*G.T.O.*)

Aerial view of the Rock. (*G.T.O.*)

The steep northern face of the Rock seen from Eastern Beach. (*G.T.O.*)

A western view of the Rock: the town is in the foreground. (*G.T.O.*)

The eastern slopes of the Rock showing the water catchments: the Caleta Palace Hotel is in the centre on the coast and the Gibraltar Beach Hotel is at the bottom right-hand corner. (*G.T.O.*)

The Upper Rock from the south. (*G.T.O.*)

A concert at St Michael's Cave. (*G.T.O.*)

(*Overleaf*) The three Moles of the harbour with Algeciras in the background. (*G.T.O.*)

A crag martin on the left and a honey buzzard. (*Charles Perez*)

Grand Casemates Gates at the entrance to the town near the Waterport. (*G.T.O.*)

The Ceremony of the Keys in Casemates Square: this is performed occasionally to commemorate the nightly closing of the gates in former times. (*G.T.O.*)

A Main Street scene. (*G.T.O.*)

Another Main Street scene outside the Exchange Building. (*G.T.O.*)

The Trafalgar Cemetery, containing many graves of members of the garrison and their families as well as those killed at Trafalgar. (*G.T.O.*)

View from the Holiday Inn: the Garrison Library is in the centre behind the trees. (*G.T.O.*)

General Eliott's monument in the Alameda Gardens. (*G.T.O.*)

The Main Street flower market: the flowers are imported from Spain and Morocco. (*G.T.O.*)

(*Above*) The Home and Mediterranean Fleets congregate in the harbour in 1939 (*The Times*)

Old and new: (*left*) an old cannon points across the airfield and the isthmus into Spain (*G.T.O.*) and (*right*) a Spanish water vendor in the 1930s.

Hotels: (*above*) the Bristol Hotel, in the town right against the background of the Rock, overlooking the harbour (*G.T.O.*) and (*below*) the Caleta Palace Hotel, in the background of this popular sandy beach. (*G.T.O.*)

normal dress for dinner but the hotel gives a feeling that black ties and long dresses would be more appropriate. It was a splendid hotel for the few British people able to afford to escape northern winters during the inter-war years. Like other older hotels it has needed to adapt to present times both in style and economics.

For families looking for warm sunshine on beaches the Gibraltar Beach Hotel (formerly known as Both Worlds) and the Caleta Palace on the eastern side of the Rock are unrivalled. The Gibraltar Beach Hotel consists of self-catering apartments standing above a sandy beach. There is a row of shops at hand selling everything necessary for catering and restaurant facilities are also available. The Caleta Palace is run on normal hotel catering lines, offering a friendly comfortable atmosphere with views out into the Mediterranean and along the Spanish coast. It stands just above Catalan Bay which provides a bathing beach and British-style bars. The hotel also has its own swimming pool and sun terrace.

The closure of the Spanish frontier in 1969 and the prevention of female workers crossing for some time before that posed a problem for all hotels. The gap was, however, largely filled with Moroccan workers who, despite some language difficulties in the early days, quickly adapted themselves in all respects.

The hotel and catering industry employs over 700 persons of all nationalities including some young people from Britain. Indirectly many other workers are largely dependent upon the tourist industry for their jobs and livelihood. The industry showed itself to be viable even with a closed frontier, but its prosperity is greatly improved with an open frontier.

The closing of the Spanish frontier had some good effects in making Gibraltarians more aware of their own resources. Previously family outings had tended to be made to Spain, but the opening of large areas of the Upper Rock to the general public led to increased awareness of Gibraltar's rich natural history as well as its military history. These resources also play a part in making Gibraltar an interesting place for tourists to visit as well as one with warmth and sunshine.

9
The Natural Heritage

Nature did not endow the limestone Rock with much soil on which crops could be grown. Goat herdsmen and vegetable growers have at certain times made a little money out of activities which might be described as agricultural, but today Gibraltar is without any agriculture and is consequently excluded from the EEC Common Agricultural Policy which causes so much worry for other members.

THE LIMESTONE MOUNTAIN

The limestone of the Rock is in itself of great interest. Like limestone elsewhere it has been eroded into both underground caves and sea caves around the coast. Within the Rock there is a constant trickle of many underground streams, which through erosion and the slow dissolution of the limestone have gradually produced caves. Within the caves themselves stalactite and stalagmite formations have resulted from the evaporation of water and the precipitation of calcite, a crystalline form of calcium carbonate. Yet another form of calcium carbonate is the chalk well known on the downlands of Britain; limestone is likewise known in Britain for its cave formation in the Mendips and the Peak District of the Pennines.

St Michael's is the largest and best known cave; it stands 900ft above sea level with a fairly small opening to the western side of the Rock. Within the opening there is an impressive dome-shaped cavern 70ft high known as the Cathedral. During World War II this was fitted out as a hospital, but never actually put into use. Now it is a place of tourist interest and is used for musical performances, to which its fine acoustics are well suited. The cave was perhaps of more natural beauty before it was developed as a tourist attraction. The cavern also has some history and folklore attached to it; in Moorish times it was well known and during the thirteenth siege in 1727 it was a hiding place for attackers. There is a story that two officers disappeared into the cave a few years before the first exploration of it in 1840 by Captain Webber-Smith, and were never seen again. No trace has ever been found of their remains, however, so it seems unlikely that they were in fact lost in the cave. From a historical point of view the sea caves are more interesting; seven of these lying north-east of Europa Point have revealed remains of pottery and jewellery from Phoenician times. The Phoenicians revered the Rock as one of the Pillars of Hercules and seem to have visited the caves in about 800 BC.

The first scientific geological study of the Rock was made in 1876 by Ramsay and Geikie, whose task was to find a fresh water supply. They failed in this, but produced a most informative study of the Rock's structure. As well as being riddled with caves they found a number of fault lines. The most marked of these is known as the main fault. It runs in a south easterly direction from near the end of South Mole in the harbour area through Windmill Hill to the sea about half a mile north of Europa Point. Standing near Europa Point looking northwards, the limestone beds of the Upper Rock can be seen to dip westwards towards the Bay of Gibraltar whilst those on Windmill Hill lower down can be seen to dip towards the Mediterranean. On the western side the limestone beds are covered by shales at their lower levels and in the area of the Alameda Gardens there are sandy soils. Wells were sunk through the sand onto the shales in Moorish times and there was a Spanish aqueduct to the town, but these wells have been brackish for several centuries.

RAINFALL AND SUNSHINE

Difficulties over water supplies on the Rock do not arise from a lack of rainfall, but rather from its slow trickling away through many little channels inside the limestone in a way which has eluded capture in quantities large enough to be useful. The average annual rainfall of 32 inches is higher than that of many places in Britain, particularly those on the eastern side of the country. Seasonal distribution is, however, an important factor, with an almost complete lack of rain in June, July and August, apart from a very occasional shower. In most years nearly all the rain falls between the beginning of November and the end of March. Snow is almost unknown, but there are sometimes heavy hailstorms.

The most striking and valuable feature of Gibraltar's climatic heritage is the abundant sunshine. Even in December there is a daily average of about five hours whilst in July the figure is eleven hours. There are, however, considerable variations in the incidence of sunshine on different parts of the Rock. The eastern side falls into the shadow of the Rock in the afternoons as the sun becomes lower in the western sky. In the town area the sun is frequently obscured by the banner cloud formed at the top of the Rock by the humid easterly wind known as the Levanter. When this blows, warm moist air from the Mediterranean is forced upwards causing condensation. In summer, particularly in August, a very heavy cloud can be formed with a humidity of over ninety per cent in the town, but rain rarely falls. August is the warmest month with an average daily mean temperature of 75°F whilst January is the coldest with a corresponding temperature of 55°F. Figures of this nature can, however, be misleading when there are wide local variations in how the weather feels; this might perhaps be described as the physiological climate as it affects the individual according to where on the Rock he is situated and the strength of the wind. On a summer morning with a Levanter blowing the town can seem hot and oppressive, but around the eastern side the same morning can seem pleasantly warm with a gentle breeze. At the southern end of the Rock the strength of the wind is an important factor. Whether from east or west there nearly always seems to be a strong breeze around this part of the Rock. In winter it can seem cold even on a sunny day, while in the town it may seem pleasantly warm. However, generally the cool breezes are more often an advantage than a disadvantage; the British garrison slowly came to take advantage of this in the location of army quarters, barracks and other establishments. The older quarters and barracks are in the town area but are now little used as such, since most establishments have moved to the southern end of the Rock. One similarity with the British climate is that westerly winds associated with

Atlantic depressions and fronts bring much of the rain. The storm tracks do not, however, extend so far south in summer. The Levanter has no counterpart in Britain, but it can be a scapegoat for human ills in Gibraltar in the same way as British weather is blamed for many things.

PLANT LIFE

Shallow alkaline soils and a hot dry season might be expected to preclude much plant growth on the Rock. On the contrary, however, plant life thrives practically everywhere except where there is either solid rock or concrete. The absence of frost except for very slight occasional ground frost is an advantage and there are many plants which can resist long drought, but would not survive frost. The Upper Rock, largely covered with trees and herbaceous shrubs, is one distinct zone for plant life. Europa Point and the area around it constitutes another zone; here strong salty winds prevent the growth of large species or those badly affected by salty air. A third distinct zone is on the eastern side of the Rock on the blown sands; here creeping plants have been naturalised to prevent the sands being washed away. A fourth zone consists of the town and the Alameda Gardens where many trees, shrubs and small plants have been cultivated.

There is much interest to be found in the study of plant life. On the Upper Rock it is surprising how trees flourish in the shallow soils and high winds. Olives predominate (although these are not fruit-bearing), alongside larger trees such as pines and eucalyptus either planted in avenues along the roads or rising above the low scrub (known as *maquis*). Fires are a hazard in the dry season as in other Mediterranean lands. Small plants which flourish include the Gibraltar candytuft, *Iberis Gibraltarica*, a native of North Africa and only naturalised in Europe on the Rock of Gibraltar. It can be grown as a garden plant in Britain but needs to be seen in Gibraltar to be properly appreciated. Bulbous and tuberous plants abound as these are well adapted to a long dry season. They include the paper-white narcissus (*Narcissus tazetta*), the asphodel (*Asphodelus microcarpus*), and the rosy-flowered onion (*Allium roseum*). The narcissus can be seen in flower in November and December, the asphodel in February

117

and March and the rosy-flowered onion a little later. Once the ground has become saturated with rain in October or November all the plants come into their own and the Upper Rock takes on a generally green appearance splashed with colourful flowers – a welcome sight for winter visitors from Britain and north-west Europe. Visitors at this time of year should of course be prepared for a few days of the rainfall which helps to generate the burgeoning plant life.

The Europa and Catalan Bay areas have more cultivated plants than the Upper Rock. Near Europa the silver ragwort (*Senecio cineraria*), the sea lavender (*Limonium spathulatum*) and the red-hot poker (*Aloe arborescens*) have become naturalised and spread themselves from cultivations. Amongst the wild flowers the sweet alyssum (*Alyssum maritimum*) grows both around Europa and on the Upper Rock. On the slopes near Catalan Bay a mesembryanthemum (*Carpobrotus acinaciforme*), has been planted and encouraged to grow over the sandy slopes. It has become naturalised together with the broom (*Cytisus linifolius*) and the *Lotus creticus*, which are leguminous plants.

The Alameda Gardens have some affinity to gardens in southern Spain in the type of plants grown, but their layout is more similar to that of English public gardens with flower beds, paths and seats. There are no lawns as these would require watering in summer and the wells in the vicinity are too saline for this purpose. The gardens are colourful in all seasons except for late summer and early autumn. When rain comes it soon brings shrubs such as hibiscus, plumbago, lantana, datura and bougainvillea into bloom. Later, smaller plants such as irises and asphodels come into flower. Overhead shade is provided by cypress trees and a few pines including the Aleppo pine. The hillside site of the gardens provides the ideal spot to take a seat and watch the sunset behind the hills to the west of Algeciras. Some private gardens, too, have similar plants to those in the Alameda Gardens and there is a nursery in the Alameda from which young plants can be purchased. Space on the Rock necessitates most gardens being small in size, but there are some in the town including that of the Bristol Hotel which provide shade in summer and sunny corners in winter. Climbing plants such as bougainvillea and lantana are particularly suitable; cacti are also grown as these can likewise look after themselves in dry summers.

ANIMAL LIFE

The apes are the best known mammalian species on the Rock. There is fossil evidence of large mammals in earlier times but now the apes are the only large animals living in a wild state, although they are not completely wild in the sense of fending for themselves. Since 1915 their care has been the responsibility of a commissioned officer. The animals were first brought onto the Rock by the Moors; they have become known as apes, although they should be more properly called monkeys of the species *Macaca sylvana*. There is much superstition and folklore surrounding them. During World War II Sir Winston Churchill did not take any chances over the Spanish superstition that the British will go when the apes leave the Rock. The animals were somewhat low in numbers early in the war so the British Prime Minister ordered some more to be brought from North Africa. More recently a virus infection has affected them causing some deaths. They are a great tourist attraction and notices are displayed warning against leaving things like cameras and wallets where they can exercise their acquisitive instincts. In the course of history they have been scapegoats for a number of misdemeanours and they are undoubtedly interested in humans and their ways. A governor was once pelted with stones.

The only other mammals are some species of rodent, but the bird life is rich in interest for ornithologists. The Barbary partridge is unique amongst resident birds in that it is not found elsewhere outside its African habitat. Its cousin the red-legged partridge lives in southern Spain but not the Barbary partridge, which was probably first brought across the Straits by the Moors. It could hardly have flown across unless previous generations were better fliers, as the present specimens cannot even fly across the isthmus without a staging post. The species thrived on the Upper Rock as a military area from which the public was excluded, so there may be some danger to the partridge now so much of the area has been opened to the public. Other resident species of birds include barn owls, wrens, warblers, blackbirds, bluetits, yellow finches, blue rock thrushes and herring gulls. Altogether about fifteen species of resident birds regularly nest in the Upper Rock. In the town sparrows abound as they do almost everywhere inhabited by man, but blackbirds being tree-dwellers are comparatively rare in the built-up areas.

Gibraltar is an outstanding place for the study of migratory birds. The three main migratory routes out of Europe in winter and back in spring are across the Bosphorus, through Italy and across the Straits of Gibraltar. The short sea crossing at the western end of the Mediterranean is particularly valuable for large birds which cannot easily cover long distances over the sea. Travel over land is less difficult, as in daytime upward thermal currents help them.

Nearly every month of the year some migration takes place. In September large flocks of honey buzzards are on their way south to be followed in October by booted eagles, marsh harriers, sparrow hawks, gannets, terns and black-headed gulls. Many smaller birds travel south in November, including finches, linnets and siskins. Some species such as gannets and crag martins use the Rock as a wintering area, but most migratory birds use it only as a staging post. There is little migration in December and January, but some late migrants will generally be still moving south in December and some early movement northwards may take place at the end of January.

Weather variations from year to year have an effect on the time of migration. Wind direction also has an effect influencing the direction in which birds come across the Straits; westerly winds drive them towards the Rock whereas easterly winds send them towards the other end of the Straits. Northward migrations generally begin in February and March, with April and May being the months of greatest activity. The season starts with the movement of large birds of prey such as kites, eagles and kestrels; these are followed by flocks of smaller birds such as finches, wheatears and warblers. The honey buzzard goes north again in April and swifts generally appear about this time; some swifts stay on the Rock but most spend the summer in Spain, or elsewhere further north, but they tend to be on the way south again by the end of July. Migratory land birds do not generally spend much time on the Rock, but heavy rains may cause them to spend longer. The effect of weather conditions both locally and further north on migrations is one of the interesting features of a study of migratory birds around the Rock.

THE SEAS AROUND THE ROCK

Land birds may not find much to eat on the Rock, depending upon their diet, but there is plenty of good fish for sea birds. There is not much commercial fishing, but for sporting fishermen the area provides variety since it is the meeting point of Atlantic and Mediterranean waters. In summer mackerel abound and during winter bonito can be caught; this is a larger fish of the same family. A blue shark weighing over 200lb was once caught far out at sea, and there is much competition over catches of stone bass. Around the rocky coasts and off the North Mole there is line fishing from the shore for bream.

The fresh breezes around the Rock and further afield provide good sailing, but currents require careful navigation in some places. Around Europa Point there is a strong race; at surface level the water flows from the Atlantic into the Mediterranean where evaporation is much higher, while at lower levels the flow is in the opposite direction and at a slower rate. This has some importance for submariners, but not for yachtsmen.

The waters around the Rock are cooler than most of the Mediterranean but between May and November the temperature in the Bay of Gibraltar generally stays above 60°F. It is some degrees higher in the middle of this period, and also in sheltered inlets around the coast. For sea bathing the Spanish Costa del Sol has the advantage, but the Rock has plenty to offer yachtsmen and also those interested in the study of birds, fish and mammals. Amongst the last dolphins are worthy of mention, and sea trips are available for the purpose of observing these active and graceful creatures.

Gibraltar is well known for its bird life, but other creatures of interest to the naturalist should not be overlooked. Lizards and snakes are both present although not in abundance; the latter can generally be described as harmless but perhaps not of great interest. In the insect world migratory butterflies provide possibilities for scientific study as well as adding colour to the natural scene on the Rock. In April or May large swarms of the Painted Lady butterfly arrive on the Rock in the course of their northward migration to Britain and elsewhere in Europe. The proper home of this butterfly is probably in North Africa where at times their numbers are so great that migration becomes a necessity.

Gibraltar provides opportunities for environmental studies which would hardly be expected from a view of the limestone as it appears from the sea or the air. A study of birds leads to knowledge of how their life is affected by winds, trees, other ground cover, crannies in the Rock, human habitation and the availability of plants, seeds, insects or fish for food. Studies of other features similarly tend to lead to a wider appreciation of the natural environment of the Rock as a whole. The exclusion of the general public from military areas for many years has helped towards conservation. Ensuring that greater public access does not destroy some of the features of this wealthy natural environment is one of the tasks of the Gibraltar Heritage Trust set up in 1987. The establishment of the Trust was prompted by the need to preserve old buildings and fortifications, but the natural heritage is coming to be seen as equally important.

10
The Historical Heritage

Human occupation of the Rock since the Moorish arrival in 711 has left many landmarks which can still be seen and studied. Little can be seen above ground dating from the earliest Moorish days, but their need for water from the time of their arrival leads to a study of Gibraltar's water supply as a point at which the natural heritage and the human heritage meet. We do not know how the Moors obtained water after they landed in 711. The question could indeed be a vital one in deciding whether the Moors really did land on the Rock or not. They would have needed a large amount of water for their 500 horses as well as for their 7,000 men, and this adds some weight to the contention that they land-ed some distance to the north-east on the Mediterranean coast.

THE WATER SUPPLY

After a time the Moors sank wells in the area of the Alameda Gardens and obtained water from the point at which the sands overlie the shales. This would not have been a ready source of supply, as the wells which still exist with brackish water would have taken some time to construct. The Moors also used rain water collected into underground storage tanks. At the Tower of Homage of the Moorish Castle there is a shaft-like reservoir into which rain water was drained from the roof, but this again was a much later development.

The Moors also built an aqueduct from the wells in the Alameda Gardens to carry water to the town and to the Moorish baths (now situated in the Museum). Further aque-ducts were built during the Spanish period including one from the Rosia Road area to the town. One of these, built in 1571, supplied a fountain in the town centre in the area now known as Fountain Ramp. Underground reservoirs were constructed during the seventeenth century with capacities of between 8,000 and 15,000 gallons.

The early history of the water supply illustrates the diffi-culty always experienced in Gibraltar over this question; this extended into the British period and indeed is still not an easy matter. For the first century of the British period the garrison looked after its own needs mostly by collection and storage of rain water; at the same time the civil population fended for itself by using the old Spanish supplies, brackish wells and rain water collected from roofs.

By the middle of the nineteenth century it was realised that water supplies in Gibraltar were most unsatisfactory and a Parliamentary Commission was appointed in 1863. Amongst evidence taken was a statement from the Garrison Quarter Master saying, 'the inhabitants owe nothing to the British government for the water they have had for 150 years'. Following the report of the Commission, a catchment area was established above Moorish Castle and a reservoir with the capacity for 1¼ million gallons was constructed. Sanitary Commissioners were set up in 1865 entrusted with the task of laying on a piped water supply to the town. In 1868 groundwater exploration on the isthmus resulted in wells being sunk and water pumped to the reservoirs near Moorish Castle. These wells quickly became brackish and thus unsuitable for drinking purposes, but the water continued to be used for washing and other sanitary purposes. This was the beginning of today's system of a dual water supply. Fresh water is now available for both washing and drinking, but a sea water supply is used for flushing toilets, street cleaning and firefighting.

Construction of the present day waterworks began in 1898. By 1900 four reservoirs had been excavated inside the Rock making storage capacity available for 5 million gallons of water. The reservoirs were lined with bricks and cement in order to render them impervious, and water was fed into them from catchment areas on the north-western slopes of the Rock.

In 1903 the City Engineer inaugurated work on catchments on the eastern side of the Rock built on a system which was probably unique. The sandy slopes had seemed an unlikely area for water collection, but a process was developed of driving vertical supports into the sand and putting timber cross members onto them. Iron sheets were attached to the timbers to make a 'roof' on which water could be collected; this was in turn covered with a thin layer of cement and thus the catchment area was begun.

Today this covers some 30 acres and can be seen for many miles. Water from the catchments flows into large channels which run laterally; these convey the water into a tunnel which cuts right through the Rock from east to west. There are now thirteen reservoirs with a total storage capacity of some 16 million gallons.

The idea of finding water below the isthmus was abandoned after the survey by Ramsay and Geikie in 1876, but in 1933 the possibility was considered again and as a result of drilling two aquifers were found; an upper unconfined one bore fresh water whilst the lower confined one contained brackish water. The upper one had probably been missed in the survey by Ramsay and Geikie, but nearly sixty years later it was developed to provide fresh water and still does so. The water is pumped to a pumping station at the foot of the Rock known as Hesse's station near Landport Gate. It is then carefully analysed for chloride content to avoid excessive pumping which would lead to an unacceptable level of salinity, through seepage of sea water.

A third source of water in use since 1956 has been the various distillation plants which use sea water. The first of these was placed near Hesse's Pumping Station, but this was not particularly successful. Between 1964 and 1976 water was distilled at the King's Bastion Electricity Generating Station using waste heat and in 1969 a long tube multi-stage flash distiller was commissioned just north of the Rock. These plants are no longer used and water is now distilled from two multi-stage flash distillers commissioned in 1984 using waste heat from the new Waterport generating station. Together they have a capacity of nearly 300,000 gallons a day and therefore in theory could be used to fill Gibraltar's reservoirs once every two months. The water is, however, blended with well water in a tank at Hesse's Pumping Station before filling the reservoir.

Distillation plants have generally been successful when they have used waste heat, but high fuel oil prices have rendered the system expensive in plants designed for water distillation only. As a seaport Gibraltar has the further possibility of importing water by tanker when threatened with a shortage. At one time water was imported from as far away as Tyneside in the north of England, but usually it has been obtained from nearer at hand. Today the facility is available for tanker water near the Waterport distillation plant, so that it can easily be discharged whenever required.

Water from natural streams running through the Rock still escapes into the sea without any usable supply having been located. In 1889 Major Tullock of the Royal Engineers put forward the theory that at some point fresh water should be found resting on heavier sea water before flowing out to sea. However, the use of both tracer dyes and infra-red photography in the period following World War II have failed to locate any large outflow. Previously the excavation of some thirty miles of tunnels did not come upon any source so it seems unlikely that the Rock will ever provide a source of water in usable quantities.

The diagram in Appendix III gives an outline of the circulation of the potable water system. The separate sea water system is based upon two intakes, one at the north-west and the other at the south-west of the Rock; the water from these intakes is pumped into reservoirs at different locations around the Rock. The biggest problem arises from corrosion in the old cast-iron mains, which are in the process of being replaced with more resistant plastic materials.

It is always difficult to be sure of the uniqueness of any situation, but there can be few places requiring as wide a range of skills as Gibraltar from water engineers in dealing with different types of supply. There can also be few places where an ordinary visitor could find so much of interest woven around a necessity of life normally taken for granted.

MAIN STREET AND THE TOWN

Many visitors on day visits from ships or from Spain do not go far beyond Main Street. This is not as unenterprising as it might seem for there is so much to see in and around the area. Shopping is of course an attraction, but there are also plenty of small lanes to explore and places to sit and watch the world go by.

Casemates Square provided the traditional entrance to Main Street from Waterport Wharf, but there are many other ways into it through smaller streets. Casemates Square itself, an area with much history, has been at the centre of recent controversy about the destruction of old buildings. The Grand Casemates on the south side of the square still stand bearing an inscription dated 1817 referring to Sir George Don, the lieutenant-governor at the time. On the west side of the square are the old gates through which traffic enters and leaves the town. Inscriptions on the gates dated 1824 and 1883 respectively refer to the Earl of Chatham and General Adye. The Earl was governor in 1824, but Sir George Don was effectively in command for most of his period in Gibraltar between 1814 and 1832. The gates stand on the site of an old water gate, which dates from a time when the sea came up to this point before the harbour works were built out into the sea.

An archway at the north-east corner of the square leads to the old Landport Gate. This stands in the style of its reconstruction after the siege of 1727, when much damage to the area was done by Spanish bombardment. The Ceremony of the Keys still takes place several times a year with much military pomp to commemorate the custom of the nightly locking of the gates to the town. Some governors are said to have left the keys under their pillows to be sure that all would be well for the night.

The purpose of the casemates was for the storage of supplies for the garrison, but the buildings on the north side of the square are the only ones in their original form. On the west side of the square government offices have replaced the casemates, and commercial buildings now occupy the east side. On the south side various old buildings have been demolished to make way for a multi-storey car park. This has caused much heated argument, but the opening of the frontier has added to acute difficulties over parking. Gibraltar is in a dilemma – the heritage of old buildings needs to be protected, but the tourist industry requires car parks and modern hotels and other buildings if visitors are to come to appreciate those very historical gems.

At the northern end of Main Street leading off Casemates Square, shops selling items subject to high customs duties elsewhere such as watches, binoculars, alcoholic drinks and tobacco are much in evidence as well as a number of banks. A number of the shops for goods which are duty-free or carrying low duty go back to the days when most of Gibraltar's visitors came ashore from ships, but many of the banks are a recent development following the re-opening of the frontier; even the banks which were there previously have been refurbished and modernised. Narrow streets leading off Main Street to right and left have names such as Turnbull's Lane and Parliament Lane, but most of the shops and commercial houses have Gibraltarian names such as Stagnetto, Basadone, Galliano and Sacerello. Some of the narrow streets were originally routes for hauling supplies and equipment up the Rock. Many of the lanes are called Ramps or Steps prefixed by a name. The steps are often deep from front to back making them suitable in former times for pack animals, but for two-legged humans they can be distinctly uncomfortable!

The importance of Gibraltar's engineers and artillery is represented in the names of Engineer Lane and Cannon Lane. Each lane had a house once occupied by the commanding officers of the respective branches of the services. Engineer House as it was called was demolished to make room for a car park. It was built by General Eliott's engineer, Sir William Green, who did much to improve and maintain the defences of Gibraltar, and the house was a good example of the solid architecture of the time. The demolition caused an outcry, which was a substantial spur towards a more conservationist approach to Gibraltar's architectural heritage.

About half-way along the mile length of Main Street there stands the Exchange Building. This once housed the Exchange Committee which attracted such adverse comment from General Gardiner in the middle of the nineteenth century. Now the upper floor accommodates the Gibraltar Assembly whilst below there is a place for refreshments which can be taken outside onto the pavement. This is a good area from which to observe the bustling life of Main Street, made even more colourful by flower sellers.

At the back of the Exchange Building is situated the modern Piazza, an area for sitting out surrounded by refreshment booths. At the other end of the Piazza is the City Hall, originally a mansion built by Aaron Cardozo at the beginning of the nineteenth century. The building has much history attached to it, studied in great detail by Dorothy Ellicott and her late husband. As the name suggests, it was once the City Hall; today it serves as government offices, but it could well have a future use more in keeping with its former days. In its time it has been the Gibraltar Garrison Club, where spectacular balls were held, and Connaught House, when the Duke resided in Gibraltar for a short period in 1875–76. At the time of the Duke of Kent's governorship at the beginning of the nineteenth century there was a whipping post here for unruly soldiery. The whole area is now called John Mackintosh Square, but was formerly called Commercial Square and known colloquially as 'the Jews' Market'. In the period between the world wars there were many stalls selling bric-a-brac, *objets d'art* and almost anything saleable. The whole area has so much history attached to it that the modern Piazza hardly seems to do it justice.

To the south of the Exchange Building is the Roman Catholic Cathedral of St Mary the Crowned, on the site of the old Moorish mosque. Some remains of the old mosque are still visible and at one time soon after the Spanish capture of Gibraltar from the Moors in 1462, the mosque was used as the cathedral. Much damage was done to the building during the sieges of 1727 and 1779–83 during the British period and the cathedral had to be rebuilt after 1783.

Main Street widens opposite the Cathedral of St Mary the Crowned, but a narrower section leads up to the entrance to Cathedral Square, named after the Anglican Cathedral of the Holy Trinity laid down in 1825 and consecrated in 1838. It contains the grave of Sir George Don who was the governor at the time of its building. It is less impressive in style than the other cathedral, but it has some slightly Moorish appearance about it.

From Cathedral Square southwards another narrow stretch of Main Street passes the Law Courts on the east side; this is yet another building dating from Sir George Don's time with a pleasant garden in front. The street widens a little further south where King's Chapel and the Convent stand on the west side. The Chapel was originally part of the Convent and was the only place of Anglican worship in Gibraltar until the Cathedral of the Holy Trinity was built. The Convent has been the residence of British Governors since the Rock has been British. It became the residence of the senior British officer in 1704, but the Franciscans were not expelled until 1712. The Franciscans established themselves in Gibraltar in 1480 and the convent was built during the sixteenth century, but the present façade was rebuilt in the nineteenth century in the Gothic style used for some buildings in Britain at the time. The name 'convent' is interesting in that it was retained after the friars had left, but it apparently displeased King Edward VII on whose orders the name was changed in 1908. He seem to have been uneasy about one of his overseas governors living in a convent and ordered the name to be changed to Government House. Thus it was known until 1943, but then his grandson King George VI, staying in Gibraltar on his way to visit his troops in North Africa, ordered the historical name to be restored.

From the Convent to Southport Gates at the southern entrance to the town, Main Street is wider and less crowded. Shops on the east side represent a variety of trades, and on the opposite side are some old army quarters, John Mackintosh Hall and Ince's Hall. This hall used to be an army recreation centre with a theatre within it, but has now been handed over to civilian use and events such as drama festivals are held there. John Mackintosh Hall is a much more modern building, opened in 1964 and built on the site of the old Ordnance Depot which suffered severe damage in 1951 when a lighter containing ammunition exploded alongside a supply ship, the *Bedenham*. This accident caused more damage in Gibraltar than the air raids of World War II. Thirteen people were killed and many more were injured.

Main Street ends at Southport Gates, which consist of three arches going through Charles V Wall. The original arch bears the Spanish Royal Arms above it, the second arch was made in 1883 and a third arch was made in 1967. The Trafalgar Cemetery lies just outside the town between the entrance to Main Street and Prince Edward Road. This road provides another way into the town through Prince Edward Gate constructed through Charles V Wall in 1790. The Prince, the fourth son of George III, was serving in the garrison at the time as a young officer; later as Duke of Kent he became Governor in 1802.

Between Prince Edward Road and Main Street runs Town Range, containing some of the oldest army buildings which date from the eighteenth century. A few have been demolished, but the remaining buildings are all worthy of preservation. Some buildings are presently used by the Government Education Department as school rooms and staff rooms but the buildings still bear some of their old inscriptions. Opposite Forty Steps which lead down from Prince Edward Road to Town Range there is the inscription 'Officers' Barracks No I', but adjacent to the steps there is a more impressive Georgian-style building designated 'Officers' Quarters No. II'. Similar inscriptions exist on old army buildings along the street northwards to the square known as Governor's Parade.

At one time Governor's Parade was an open space used for military ceremonies, but now it is surrounded by buildings, mostly dating from the nineteenth century. These include the Presbyterian Church of Scotland at the entrance from Town Range; this is a reminder of the long association of Scottish regiments with the Rock. The building too is in a style of stone construction which would not be out of place in Scotland.

The eastern side of Governor's Parade is dominated by the Garrison Library, a long low building completed in 1804. It is difficult not to regret the dwarfing of this pleasing old building by the Holiday Inn opened in 1973 on the opposite side of the square. Such a hotel was needed, however, and it can at least be said that the foyer of the hotel provides a good view of the Library and the tiers of the old buildings rising above it. These can be approached by Library Steps to the north of the Library, once part of one of the old routes for taking supplies up the Rock.

The Garrison Library is remarkable not only for its collection of works about Gibraltar, some of which are unobtainable elsewhere, but for its large collection of other books including many of the great classics of English literature. The library is a private concern with a management committee but its future organisation has been under consideration for some time. It welcomes temporary members and this might in future be made a more useful source of revenue. The old building is expensive to maintain particularly from a decorative point of view, which is always a problem in Gibraltar's damp climate.

The idea of establishing a library seems to have arisen shortly after the Great Siege of 1779–83 and it interested Captain John Drinkwater who wrote the best known work on the siege after having served during it. A committee was set up in 1793 with a view to getting the British Government to support the idea; amongst other reasons put forward was that of saving members of the garrison from 'having their minds enervated and vitiated by dissipation'.

The library contains copies of the *Gibraltar Chronicle* from the early days of its publication beginning in 1801, when it started as a garrison newspaper. It is now independent and is produced in premises adjoining the Garrison Library. Other newspapers have been published in Gibraltar from time to time, but none has achieved the long term publication of the *Chronicle*; it has maintained a consistent standard of factual reporting from its early days when it achieved the distinction of being the first newspaper to publish news of the Battle of Trafalgar in 1805.

Other nineteenth-century buildings in Governor's Parade include the old Sergeants' Mess on the west side and the Theatre Royal in the north-west corner. The former is solidly built befitting sergeants whilst the latter now bears a forlorn look having been unused for many years. It is in need of friends but it is doubtful whether it could ever again be a successful theatre. However, the façade would seem worth restoration even if much behind it had to be rebuilt for use for other purposes.

A short distance from Governor's Parade on the west side of Main Street, the Gibraltar Museum complements the Garrison Library as a place to study Gibraltar's history. It boasts an impressive collection of exhibits covering both natural and human history. The entrance is in Bomb House Lane, running north from Cathedral Square, and the building incorporates both a Moorish bath house and a former residence of the Officer Commanding the Royal Army Ordnance Corps. The existence of the bath house has led to a belief that the site might have been that of the residence of Governors in Moorish times. The museum was opened in 1930, but has been greatly improved in recent years as a place to study Gibraltar's history. One of the exhibits is a scale model of the Rock as it was in 1865, a notable piece of artistic work as well as being historically valuable. The museum provides a good starting-point from which the visitor can pick out places and subjects of interest, and further study can often be made in the Garrison Library.

The buildings in Line Wall Road behind the museum, running from Cathedral Square northwards above the Line Wall, are built of solid Portland stone imported during the nineteenth century. Almost identical stone exists in Gibraltar, but getting it cut in the same style as that used for the Line Wall would have been a problem. The site of King's Bastion which did so much damage to the Spanish invasion fleet in 1782 also stands in this area quite near the museum. The building of the old power station as well as the nineteenth-century Line Wall unfortunately obscures much of the construction of the battery. Further along Line Wall Road is the American War Memorial and near this Fountain Ramp leads into John Mackintosh Square by the City Hall. Just north of the square is the Victorian-style police station, and a narrow street called Irish Town leads down to Cooperage Lane with a number of small lanes running east into Main Street. Irish Town has been connected with shipping and the commercial port for well over a century. It now also contains other offices, legal chambers, bars, restaurants and a few small shops. A recent development is a modern arcade of shops and offices between Irish Town and Main Street. In some ways modern developments detract from the historical nature of the old garrison town, but much has been preserved. As the town became unable to contain military quarters and activities, most of these have moved to the Europa area.

EUROPA AND THE SOUTHERN END OF THE ROCK

A bus service runs from the town to Europa, leaving the town by Southport Gates and following Europa Road past the Rock Hotel, the Casino, the Alameda Gardens, the Mount (the Admiral's residence) and the Naval Hospital. The lighthouse, already mentioned, is the only outstanding building in the Europa area which is worth visiting for its migratory birds and views of the Straits rather than for its buildings or historical associations. There is, however, a piece of history attached to the Shrine of Our Lady of Europa. When the Moorish kingdom in Spain had finally been defeated after the capture of Granada in 1492 a wooden image of the Virgin Mary was enshrined at the southern end of the Rock; a light was placed on the shrine for the benefit of sailors by whom it was revered. Gibraltar had been taken from the Moors back in 1462 but the Duke of Medina thought it fitting to give symbolic significance to Gibraltar when the Moors were finally expelled from Spain. The shrine was pillaged by Turkish pirates in 1540 and ransacked by British soldiers in 1704. However, the damaged image was rescued by Father Romero, who stayed behind after the British capture of the Rock. The image was sent to Spain and returned in 1866 amidst great ceremony which included a regimental band of the British Army. It was then enshrined in a chapel in the grounds of the Little Sisters of the Poor at Europa. Later, in 1968, the image was placed in a shrine made for it out of the remains of the Moorish mosque at Europa.

Most of the Europa area and Windmill Hill above it is used for military quarters, training and recreation, all of which leave little room for other development. However, the provision of a good restaurant and a covered-in area for viewing the Straits near the lighthouse could be beneficial to the tourist industry. An older building of some interest is Governor's Cottage situated on the south-eastern side of the area. It was constructed for Governors as a summer residence in 1805 after the yellow fever epidemic of 1804; it is no longer used for this purpose and might be put to some other use if the army could relinquish it. It used to have a fine garden and some of this might be rehabilitated.

A tunnel runs north-westwards from Europa, leading to Little Bay and Camp Bay which have been developed as areas for bathing, water sports and other recreational activities. Another shorter tunnel leads from Camp Bay to the area around Rosia Bay, where in 1805 *HMS Victory* came into port with Nelson's body aboard after the Battle of Trafalgar. The area needs both to be preserved and developed as a tourist attraction; the old naval hospital, Parson's Lodge, the 100-ton gun of Napier Battery just north-west of the bay and the bay itself all merit the conservationists' attention. The 100-ton gun is still in place and is an interesting ancient guardian of the Straits, although it never saw action against an enemy. It was a muzzle-loading gun with a rate of fire of one round of 2,000 pounds every four minutes; loading, traversing and elevation were operated by steam. At a demonstration in 1902 the charge failed to fire the projectile, which had to be retrieved by a slim gunner crawling down the barrel and attaching a cable with which the shot could be winched out. Happily for later generations of gunners, breech-loading guns became standard shortly after this event; these included the 6-inch and 9.2-inch guns which can still be seen on the Upper Rock.

THE UPPER ROCK

The cable car provides a good means of visiting the Upper Rock. It runs from a station near the Alameda Gardens to a point at the middle of the Upper Rock formerly occupied by a signal station. From here there are excellent views to the east into the Mediterranean and westwards through the Straits. The station is a good point from which to start walking around the Upper Rock amongst the low-growing trees and other colourful vegetation which supports much bird life.

From St Michael's Cave, a few hundred yards south of the cable car station, a walk can be taken to Jews' Gate standing at the southern end of the Upper Rock just above Windmill Hill. From here a path via Mediterranean Steps leads up the eastern side to the top of the Rock near O'Hara's Battery. The whole scene is one of great tranquillity in contrast to the busy town, dockyard, airport and roads at lower levels. There is, however, a reminder of the Rock's fortress role in the 9.2-inch gun mounted at O'Hara's Battery. This *prima donna* of generations of coast defence gunners is something well worth preservation as part of the Rock's history, although the greatest battles were fought with cannon.

Walking northwards from O'Hara's Battery it is possible to join the cable car for a return to the Alameda at a station called Apes Den. This is about half-way between the two terminus stations and, as the name suggests, is a place where the apes can frequently be seen. The Apes Den station lies between Charles

V Wall to the south and the ruins of the old Moorish Wall to the north. The former was built after the raid by Turkish pirates in 1540 whilst the latter was part of the Moorish fortifications built in the twelfth century. It formed part of the whole fortified area around the castle. Also near the Apes Den station is Healy's Mortar – a weapon carved out of stone during the great siege which was designed to shower rocks and stones onto the ground below to inconvenience any landing parties. Fortunately, there was no landing and the weapon was not used, as it might have been more dangerous to the defenders than the attackers with its inevitable inaccuracy.

A walk northwards past the Old Moorish Wall passes near Devil's Gap Battery, which can be visited and examined with its 6-inch guns still in place. These weapons were brought into service at the beginning of the present century and were standard coast defence equipment during the two world wars – the maids of all work of coast defence. The guns of Devil's Gap were fired on occasion during World War I at German submarines or suspected submarines. By World War II, however, the passage through the Straits was almost invariably made underwater.

Most of the Upper Rock defences from Devil's Gap Battery southwards have for the past hundred years been concerned with the Straits, but the northern defences have a much longer and more active history. Here fortifications have been built since early Moorish times, but some of these have been covered by later building. The area was somewhat neglected during World War I and the years thereafter when Spanish neutrality was assumed, but the rise to power of Franco and his association with Hitler and Mussolini led to a rebuilding of defences in the north; some of the older works such as the galleries of the Great Siege were once again found useful.

The oldest defences around the keep of the Moorish Castle ran right down the northern end of the Rock to the sea and would have been formidable against attackers across the isthmus. The weapons of the time were mainly longbows from which arrows could be rained down upon attackers from behind the walls of the castle. A look southwards, however, shows how the castle was vulnerable from that side; this became particularly apparent to the Moors after the unsuccessful attack by Alfonso XI in 1333. By the time a further attack was made in 1349 much work had been carried out and most of the works which can be seen today, including the present tower, had been built.

The last great episode in the history of the castle itself occurred after the Moors had been expelled in 1462, when there was a dispute between Henry IV of Castile and the Duke of Medina. The Duke gave up the Rock under protest, but recaptured it in 1467 after the governor, Esteban de Villacreces, had resisted for five months in the keep of the castle.

The northern defences were not seriously tested again until after the British were in possession of the Rock. The capture was a seaborne affair, but a Spanish attempt at recapture later in the year 1704 was based on an attempt to outflank the northern defences by using a path up the steep eastern slopes. The defences were in better shape by the time the thirteenth siege was started in 1727, and before the Great Siege of 1779–83 much work had been done on both the northern defences and the seaward defences. The latter have in many cases been obscured by subsequent building, but the northern defences based originally on Willis's Lines are still in a good state of preservation. The Galleries are the best known defences of the siege although they were not started until 1782 in an attempt to get a gun to the Notch – a point on the north face of the Rock. Whilst works were going on, the holes blown in the side of the tunnel for ventilation were found to be useful for cannon, although this had not been the original idea. Eventually the tunnelling reached a point below the Notch now known as St George's Hall, but this was not reached until after the siege was over. The Galleries now go right through to the eastern side of the Rock and provide some magnificent views through the openings. In World War II the galleries were once again part of the defences, but the northern defences would have been unlikely to be directly assaulted. If Spain had not remained neutral an airborne attack following a blockade would have been far more likely and a much more difficult tactic to defeat.

The northern defences are of interest not only to holiday-makers but also to students of Moorish history, military history and Anglo-Spanish relations. The defences span a history of weapons from bows and arrows through a long period of cannon and gunpowder to modern high explosives and airborne assault. Fortunately, the preservation of these defences is not threatened by other developments such as hotels and housing to the same extent as other old defences of Gibraltar, but the keep of the Moorish Castle would benefit from some conservation work. Lower down the slopes old Moorish walls are covered by housing, but outside the town restoration work could be carried out on the ladder of batteries and bastions going down to Hesse's Bastion by the water pumping station. Restoration where possible can at least make up for some of the destruction that has already taken place; happily in recent years there has come a realisation both in Gibraltar and in Britain of the need for a positive approach to Gibraltar's heritage.

THE HERITAGE CONFERENCE

In February 1985 a conference was held at the National Army Museum in London under the chairmanship of Lord Boyd-Carpenter – a descendant of Sir Robert Boyd who was present during the Great Siege and subsequently governor in succession to General Eliott. The opening speaker was HRH The Duke of Gloucester, who has continued to take an interest in Gibraltar's heritage and other speakers included former Governors, Gibraltar's Chief Minister and a number of persons concerned with heritage works and tourism. There were distinguished contributions from experts on conservation, architecture and history. The conference reached some constructive conclusions, and one outcome has been the setting up of the Friends of the Gibraltar Heritage Society under the presidency of HRH The Duke of Gloucester. The society is concerned with the raising of funds, advancing interest in Gibraltar's character and history and helping to protect its historic monuments.

One speaker at the conference described Gibraltar's architecture interwoven with military walls, gates and bastions as being of World Heritage status. He may have gone a little too far in deeming it as precious as Angkor Wat in Cambodia. Angkor Wat was lost in tropical forests and rediscovered as a remarkably well-preserved ruin, whereas Gibraltar's history is very much alive today. The two cannot, therefore, be preserved in the same sort of way; in Gibraltar a balance has to be established between modern hotels and old architecture, between housing for Gibraltarians and old walls and bastions, and between preserving the facades of Main Street and the needs of modern commerce and banking. The last is a growing industry and there might be a future in sponsorship of certain aspects of Gibraltar's heritage by the banks; it is in their interest for Gibraltar to develop a more sophisticated tourist industry based more on intellectual pursuits, particularly during the winter. The conversion of old buildings into hotels and the limitation of the height of buildings are other possible solutions identified by the Heritage Conference. However, therein lies a conflict of interest: hotels need to be profitable, which in a place as small as Gibraltar tends to require tall buildings, and some may have to be on sensitive sites.

The Heritage Conference provided stimulus to the setting up of the Gibraltar Heritage Trust, and The Friends of the Gibraltar Heritage Society can play a continuing role in raising funds and persuading commercial and other organisations to provide help. Amongst those that do contribute towards the interest in historical heritage, the Gibraltar Post Office deserves a mention. Much effort is put into the design of stamps related to Gibraltar's history, and commemorative issues are frequently produced for anniversaries of important events. The Post Office itself is an imposing building in Main Street built in 1858. It was originally under the British Postmaster General, but became the Gibraltar Post Office with local control in 1886. There is an active Gibraltar Philatelic Society established in its present form in 1965.

Gibraltar can be likened to other small states in Europe which rely largely upon their heritage and natural environment for their economic prosperity. There is, however, the important point that Gibraltar is presently a British colony which has great emotional significance for Spain. In Spanish eyes it is a colonial enclave on Spanish territory. It happens that there are close similarities between Gibraltar and Spanish enclaves on North African territory such as Ceuta just across the Straits, but there is a great Spanish reluctance to admit this.

11
Small States and Colonial Enclaves

Four states in Europe can usefully be considered alongside Gibraltar with regard to the possibility of Gibraltar functioning as a small state within the EEC. This would require agreement between Britain, Spain and Gibraltar, recision of the Treaty of Utrecht and the drawing up of a new treaty compatible with EEC relationships.

The four states are Andorra, San Marino, Monaco and Liechtenstein. Andorra stands high up in the Pyrenees between France and Spain with an area of 180 square miles and a population of 42,000, but only about 5,000 are Andorrans. San Marino has an area of 24 square miles and a population of 22,000. It is surrounded by Italian territory in the vicinity of Rimini, which lies on the Adriatic coast. Monaco has a minute area of about ¾ square mile and a population of 27,000, of whom only about 4,000 have Monegasque citizenship. Liechtenstein has an area of 61 square miles and a population of 27,000. It lies between Austria and Switzerland and like Andorra is in mountainous country. All four states, like Gibraltar, rely heavily on tourism, but they differ widely from each other. They have a high degree of independence which has in each case been respected over a long period of history. The degree of independence differs and they are all reliant on friendly help from their neighbours, particularly in matters concerning customs controls and currency. Their history differs greatly, but it is worth considering each in turn with a brief historical background.

ANDORRA
Hannibal had to fight the Andosians, who were presumed to have been the Andorrans, on his way to attack the Romans. However, nothing much is known about Andorra until the Middle Ages. Amongst legendary and folklore tales it is certain that Charlemagne's troops drove the Moors out of this area of

the Pyrenees; later the area came under the Count of Urgel. The count ceded his possessions in Andorra to the Bishop of Urgel in 954 and the bishop gradually built up a temporal fief over the Valleys of Andorra. The arrangement was a feudal one and the bishop granted a tenure to the lords of Caboet. Through a series of marriages – one of which was disapproved by the bishop – the tenure under the bishop became vested in the Compte de Foix in the thirteenth century. There was nearly war between them, but in 1288 an agreement was made establishing that the Compte de Foix held his seignorial prerogatives in fief from the bishop. Gradually the counts established a position of holding their office as equals of the bishop. At the end of the sixteenth century when Henry of Navarre became King of France, the estates of the counts became joined to the French Crown. Today the President of the Republic is the successor in title of the Crown and holds the position formerly held by the counts. The position of the bishop is unchanged and thus he is one of the Joint Princes with the President of France. The princes each appoint a delegate and the two of them are in effect the rulers of Andorra. There is, however, a General Council elected by adult suffrage, which is in charge of the administration of the state, subject to the authority of the Permanent Delegates. The legal system operates through tribunals with an appeal to an Appeals Judge who is appointed for life by each of the Joint Princes in turn. In civil matters there is a further appeal to a Superior Tribunal of Andorra sitting in Perpignan, France, or to the Superior Tribunal of the Mitre of Urgel, dependent upon the subject in dispute.

The whole system has the appearance of one likely to cause much confusion, but in practice it appears to work well, having been established for so long. The Franco/Spanish flavour is epitomised by two post offices – one for France and one for Spain. The economy is partly reliant on agriculture, but tourism is of much greater importance with both summer mountain resorts and winter skiing.

SAN MARINO

The Republic of San Marino differs greatly from Andorra in its form of government. The foundation of the state probably dates back to the beginning of the fourth century when Christians were being persecuted by the Roman Emperor Diocletian. A Dalmatian stone cutter named Marino, who was a Christian, is thought to have sought and obtained refuge on or near Mount Titanus after leaving Rimini on the coast where he was working. When the news spread of the area of refuge others took to it and a community was formed.

The first documentary evidence of it is dated 885 and concerns a dispute between the Abbot of San Marino and the Bishop of Rimini. The dispute was settled by a court granting certain lands to San Marino. A republican constitution was developed by about the year 1000 and San Marino was recognised as a small sovereign state by Pope Paul III in 1549. Garibaldi took refuge in San Marino in 1849 and the state maintained a neutrality in two world wars. Heavy damage was, however, unfortunately caused by an Allied bombardment in World War II.

The government of the state is today based on a Grand Council of sixty members. This elects two Captains-Regent at six-monthly intervals to run the government of the country. There are colourful ceremonies when this takes place in April and October. The economy of San Marino is based upon wheat, wine and tourism. The state coined money until 1943, but the currency is now the Italian lira and the language spoken is Italian. There are strong ties to the Roman Catholic church, so as in the case of Gibraltar there are both linguistic and religious links with a large neighbour but there is no doubt about San Marino's political independence.

LIECHTENSTEIN

The Principality of Liechtenstein is on territory acquired in 1712 by Duke Hans Adam von Liechtenstein, and was made an Imperial Principality in 1718. It was formally recognised by Napoleon in 1806 and made a state of the Rhenish League, but left the German federation in 1866. It has remained independent since that time and was neutral in both world wars. Since 1921 there has been a democratic constitution based upon the Swiss model and a customs union with Switzerland was formed in 1924. The capital Vaduz is a hub of communication both for the principality and for Austria and Switzerland. The economy is based on wine production in the sunny upper Rhine valley and on tourism; for the latter there are both warm sunny summer resorts and good ski slopes for winter sports. The principality does depend on Switzerland in matters such as currency and postal services, but Liechtenstein has a flourishing economy of its own. As in Gibraltar, banking plays a part in this.

MONACO

The Principality of Monaco has been in the hands of the Grimaldi family since the end of the thirteenth century; the present ruler Prince Rainier III is the thirty-third descendant of the founder who took the fortress of Monaco in 1297. Monaco's history goes back to the Roman era and perhaps to Phoenician times, but its present situation can be traced to the twelfth century when the Genoese established their dominion over Monaco. They built towers and ramparts, and the Citadel of the Rock – which contains the Prince's palace and government buildings – dates from this time. Like the Rock of Gibraltar the Rock of Monaco has played a great part in its defensive history.

Today Monaco falls naturally into three parts – Monaco Town, La Condamine and Monte Carlo. The last, the newest development at the east end of the principality, is perhaps the best known part through its casino. The area was covered by an olive grove until the middle of the nineteenth century when Monaco needed to find a way to make a living. Monaco Town stands at the west end of the principality and contains the cathedral, the public library and other culturally interesting places as well as the Prince's palace. In the centre La Condamine contains the harbour and the Zoological Gardens.

The existence of Monaco as an independent state today can be partly attributed to its having a long line of skilful rulers who have steered it from becoming too closely associated with outside disputes. Prince Charles III (1856–89), who built Monte Carlo, played a leading part in more recent times. Economically Monaco depends largely upon its tourist trade and this could not function without French goodwill. Relations with France are governed by a treaty of 1918 and various other agreements under which France has guaranteed the rights of the Princes to exercise sovereignty in conformity with the political, military and economic interests of France. Succession to the principality must be by a Monegasque or French subject and secession of the principality can only be to France. Briefly, Monaco can be said to be bound to France rather than subject to it. French currency is used but from time to time Monegasque currency is issued with the agreement of the French Government. Monaco stamps have been well known to philatelists ever since the first – and now very valuable – issue was made under the authority of Prince Charles III in 1885.

SMALL STATE PHILOSOPHY

All the small states considered above have something to offer in terms of possibilities for Gibraltar's future. Andorra shows how an unusual arrangement between a Spanish bishop and the President of France can provide for the functioning of a small state. San Marino and Liechtenstein show how small states can be largely independent democracies when given just a little support from outside. Monaco is an example of a small state having a good working arrangement with a large neighbour and in doing so achieving economic viability in a very small area by prudent use of resources.

There are other small states worthy of study, including the Channel Islands, where Jersey gives us an example of an arrangement which has worked well. It was separated from the Duchy of Normandy early in the thirteenth century and has a high degree of independence under the British Crown. A similar association of Gibraltar with Britain would not, however, be acceptable to Spain. At the same time a solution along the lines of Andorra would not be acceptable to Gibraltarians. There may, however, be some way in which an independent Gibraltar could be made acceptable to Spain. The main problems are the colonial past of Gibraltar and hurt Spanish feelings persisting ever since the Treaty of Utrecht.

Since World War II colonialism has become an anathema to the world in general. The British Empire was by no means an unmitigated evil, and Britain has generally shown both statesmanship and generosity in arrangements for bringing former colonies to

144

nationhood. A much more usual situation has, however, been one in which there have not been conflicting claims to territory as in the case of Spain and Gibraltar. There are, however, a few other cases worth mentioning, namely the Falkland Islands, Hong Kong and the Spanish enclaves in North Africa of Ceuta and Melilla. All of these cases are related to a colonial type of situation, but all are different. The Falkland Islands for instance, are separated from neighbouring Argentina by 300 miles of sea, whereas the other places are contiguous like Gibraltar. Where there is a colonial past, ambitions of territorial aggrandisement can spread quite a long way offshore, and mention has even been made of the Canary Islands over which several countries might make claims without any intrinsic merit.

THE FALKLAND ISLANDS

The Falkland Islands are unlike Gibraltar in many respects but there is an Anglo-Spanish background to the dispute with Argentina. The islands consist of two main islands – East and West Falkland – and about 340 smaller islands, some of which are no more than offshore masses of rock. The total area is some 4,700 square miles and the population around 2,000 persons apart from servicemen. Physically, the islands strongly resemble the Western Isles of Scotland, and in latitudes of between 51° and 53°S the islands are just a few degrees nearer the equator than the Outer Hebrides, which are situated between latitudes 57° and 59°N. The 60°W meridian passes through the middle of the islands, which are over 8,000 miles from Britain.

The events of the conflict between Britain and Argentina during 1982 are well known. Briefly, the Argentinian military dictator, General Galtieri, thought wrongly and tragically that the British were not sufficiently interested in the islands, or the people of them, to respond with force to a surprise attack. The Argentinians were defeated by a combination of well-planned strategy and out-standing courage of the forces in very difficult fighting conditions; the operations lasting over two months were finally completed during the Falkland's winter in June. The Argentinians although defeated declined to declare hostilities at an end and still expected Britain to negotiate over the sovereignty of the islands.

There are many difficulties concerning the question of sovereignty and it is worth briefly considering the history of the case. The discovery of the islands is generally thought to have been by John Davis, an Elizabethan navigator from England, in 1592. A number of French settlements were established in the eighteenth century and the islands named Isles Maloines after St Malo from where many south seas expeditions set forth. In 1764 a fort was established at Port Louis by de Bougainville – an energetic French explorer, whose name was perpetuated in the ubiquitous tropical and sub-tropical shrub bougainvillea. There was a Spanish protest and in 1767 de Bougainville handed over the colony to Spain in a friendly manner, as it was considered to be in their area of influence. A short time earlier in 1765, unbeknown to the French and Spanish, the British had landed on the islands and claimed them in the name of George III. During the next few years there was much argument between Britain and Spain over possession of the islands and for a time both British and Spanish settlements existed. In 1774 the British left although still claiming the islands for George III. Then the islands were effectively under the control of Spanish governors until 1806 and became known as Las Malvinas. The Spanish governor left in 1806 and Spanish jurisdiction lapsed in the course of revolution in her South American colonies. In 1816 the Rio de la Plata (later Argentina) emerged and this state claimed the possession of all Spanish territories in the area including Las Malvinas. Formal rights of possession were claimed in 1820 and an Argentinian governor was appointed in 1823. In 1828 Vernet was appointed governor and set about establishing a settlement of some ninety persons of various nationalities including British, Spanish, Portuguese, Dutch and French. He himself was of French birth, but he had become South American by naturalisation.

The appointment of Vernet led to a British protest in Buenos Aires on the grounds that the islands were British through earlier colonisation. The matter remained unresolved and at the end of 1832 two British naval vessels arrived to take control. At this time the islands were in a turbulent state and a temporary governor, Mestivier, had been murdered earlier in 1832. After some further turbulence British control was established over the islands and in

1842 a formal declaration was made to the islanders in the name of Queen Victoria to the effect that Her Majesty's Government would look after the islands. Thereafter the usual pattern of British colonial government was developed in the islands including in recent years elected majorities on the Executive and Legislative Councils. Historically General Galtieri's incursion in 1982 can be seen as a reversion to the practices of 150 years earlier when various countries sent forces to occupy the Falkland Islands. There was, however, by 1982 both a long established civil population and a general acceptance by civilized countries that force is not to be used in this manner.

The proceedings before the United Nations Security Council connected with the Falkland dispute led to an examination of the question of sovereignty and how it is acquired. This has some bearing on Spanish claims to Gibraltar so it is worth considering the meaning of 'sovereignty' in international law. There have been a number of definitions by international lawyers, but an easily understood explanation of the term is: 'the supreme power of the state over its territory and inhabitants and independence of any external authority'. Methods of acquiring sovereignty recognised by international law are cession, occupation, accretion, subjugation and prescription. The first four methods are fairly straightforward and as far as Gibraltar is concerned there is no doubt that most of the territory was acquired by Britain through cession by the Treaty of Utrecht. The position over the isthmus is less certain but each of the remaining four methods could be cited in support of Britain's title. The term 'prescription' gives rise to the most difficulty but it has been defined as: 'The acquisition of sovereignty over a territory through continuous and undisturbed exercise of sovereignty over it during such period as is necessary to create under the influence of historical development the general conviction that the present condition of things is in conformity with international order.'

The question of Gibraltar is almost inevitably linked in people's minds with events in the Falkland Islands. There are, however, marked differences and it is over 200 years since Spain resorted to armed force. It should also be mentioned that during the Falklands war a small group of Argentinians arrived in Spain with a view to carrying out sabotage in Gibraltar. They were quietly but quickly sent home.

HONG KONG

The similarities between Hong Kong and Gibraltar are less marked than those common to the Falklands and Gibraltar. Hong Kong is a British Colony consisting partly of an island ceded by treaty by China in 1841 and partly of territories attached to the mainland of China leased to Britain for 99 years in 1898. The lines of latitude 22° 20′ N and longitude 114° 10′ E bisect each other just north of Hong Kong Island, so it is about one third of the way around the world from Gibraltar. It has a total area, including the leased territories, of just over 400 square miles and a population of over 5.5 million people; the great majority of these are of Chinese ethnic origin from the neighbouring area around Canton. Less than ten per cent of the land area is covered by the cession of the island in 1841, which was obtained by Britain in order to have a trading base under British rule and as a suitable naval harbour in the area around China. The leasing of further territory in 1898 was for the purpose of curbing French and Russian ambitions in the area. There was, however, an unexpected increase in Chinese population in the area and some economic development instead of the area remaining simply a neutralised military zone around a naval base. During World War I and between the wars the port provided naval facilities somewhat similar to those at Gibraltar at the other end of the chain of bases. The entry of Japan into World War II in December 1941 put an end to this and there followed nearly four years of Japanese occupation. The population became reduced to about 600,000, through emigration to China, but it rose rapidly again after the Japanese had surrendered. By 1950 it exceeded two million and it has continued to rise, particularly when there has been unrest in China.

From China's point of view Hong Kong has been very useful as a point of contact economically and to some extent politically with the western world. The free economy has been beneficial for obtaining foreign currency for communist China as well as in other ways. There has, however, never been any possibility that China would allow the lease to continue beyond 1997. The return of leased territories to China has always been seen in Britain as inevitably leading to the end of British rule in the whole colony; it could not possibly be divided between ceded and leased territories. The objective of the British Government has thus been to make the best possible agreement for the people of Hong Kong, who have not had anything approaching the same degree of self-rule as Gibraltar.

The Sino-British Joint Declaration on the Question of Hong Kong was signed by the two governments in December 1984. The agreement provides for Hong Kong to become a Special Administrative Region (SAR) of the People's Republic of China on the 1 July 1997. The SAR will enjoy a high degree of autonomy with its own government and legislature, but China will be responsible for foreign affairs and defence. It was agreed that Hong Kong will retain its own social and economic systems as at present for fifty years from 1997 and that China's socialist system and policies will not be practised in the SAR. A Sino-British Land Commission and a Sino-British Joint Liaison Group were set up to oversee arrangements for the change from a British Colony to a SAR in China. Progress has, however, suffered a serious set-back as a result of the violent suppression of student unrest in China in 1989.

The agreement over Hong Kong was seen in Spain as a possible guide on how Gibraltar might be integrated into Spain. In the case of Hong Kong there has, however, never been a possibility of self-determination owing to the leasehold nature of most of its territory. There has been much less development of local political institutions, and the people of Hong Kong are Cantonese Chinese like those just across the border. In the case of Hong Kong, territory must take precedence over people for legal and historical reasons, but it is not a reason for any similar approach in the case of Gibraltar or even in the case of the Spanish enclaves in North Africa.

CEUTA AND MELILLA

Any discussion about Gibraltar and Spanish claims on it amongst well-informed persons almost inevitably leads to the question 'What about Ceuta and Melilla?' – the Spanish enclaves in North

Africa. It is, therefore, necessary to give brief consideration to these territories, which Spain claims are in a different category to the case of Gibraltar, although a more impartial observer might find the similarities more marked than the differences.

There are a number of Spanish possessions along the North African coast known as the *Presidios*, so named as they were originally penal settlements. As well as Ceuta and Melilla there are Penon ('rock') de Velez de la Gomera, Penon d'Alhuce and the Chaafferine Islands, but for present purposes only Ceuta and Melilla need to be considered. Ceuta lies almost due south of Gibraltar about 15 miles across the Straits. It has an area of 4½ square miles and a population of some 70,000 people. Melilla is about 130 miles away to the east with an area of 7½ square miles for a population of about 60,000 people. The bulk of the population in each case is of Spanish nationality, but some of these are of Moorish descent and there are also Jewish and Indian communities prominent in trade. The territories have been incorporated into metropolitan Spain, so they are not technically colonies in the same sense as Gibraltar. Thus Spain avoided reporting them as such to the UN Committee of Twenty Four in which Morocco supported Spain without raising the question of Ceuta and Melilla at the same time; other countries did so on Morocco's behalf but the question was not put before the committee in the same way.

The ports at Ceuta and Melilla are the mainstays of their economy, flourishing on low customs and excise duties, which helps their tourist trade. There are also profitable fisheries around the coasts. Both places have been Spanish for many years and are in effect Spanish towns in North Africa with a predominantly Spanish population. The Portuguese were the first nation to colonise North Africa, capturing Ceuta in 1415. In 1494, two years after the Moors had been expelled from Granada in Spain, Pope Alexander VI arbitrated between Spain and Portugal. Under this Melilla was in the Spanish zone of influence, although they did not capture it until 1497, and Ceuta remained Portuguese. Historically Ceuta is more interesting than Melilla in its association with happenings on the other side of the Straits of Gibraltar. Ceuta was known to the Phoenicians and later came under Roman control. The

Romans named it *Septa* after the seven hills around it and it later became known as Ceuta. Its Arab history reached a climax in 711 when it was the departure point for the Moorish forces under Tarik in their invasion of Spain. Ceuta continued to play an important role as a base in North Africa until captured by the Portuguese in 1415. It came under a governor sent from Portugal in 1437, and its first connection with Spain came about through the unification of the two thrones of Spain and Portugal in 1580. From this year Ceuta became under Spanish rule, as it remains today. It was seen at first as a place of importance in a Christian crusade against the Muslims of North Africa. It underwent many attacks and sieges over the centuries and like Melilla and the other *Presidios* was the subject of treaties with the Arabs. A trade and peace treaty was signed in 1767, and further treaties in 1782 and 1799 were ratified concerning the boundaries of Ceuta.

During the remainder of the eighteenth century and for the whole of the nineteenth century Ceuta and Melilla were Spanish towns in North Africa used for garrisons available to deal with disorders in the hinterland; this particularly applied in the case of the various uprisings by tribes in the Rif Mountains. The towns also had a great importance as regards trade with North Africa, and were established as free ports to rival Gibraltar. There were penal settlements in Ceuta and Melilla until 1906 and for a few more years on the offshore islands.

The Rif War of the present century lasted from 1909 to 1927, during which time the Spanish zone of Morocco became established on a firmer basis. The trading importance of Ceuta and Melilla reached its height in the period after the Rif War, but a decline set in after Morocco achieved independence in 1956. General Franco's hand was to some extent forced over the granting of independence to the Spanish zone of Morocco through the French doing so in their southern zone. He exercised considerable skill in negotiations in leaving the *Presidios* out of the deal and the territories have remained thus. King Hassan of Morocco regards them as rightly Moroccan, but he maintained friendly relations with Franco and has continued thus with subsequent Spanish governments. Franco's experience as a junior officer in North Africa assisted him considerably in negotiating with Morocco.

151

During 1986–87 there was some unrest amongst the Muslim community in Melilla. This arose partly out of alleged slowness by the Spanish authorities in registering those Muslim citizens entitled to Spanish nationality under the Aliens Law of 1985. The task of registration relates to Moroccan inhabitants of Melilla, who constitute about one-third of the population of 70,000. By no means all these are entitled to registration but this does not prevent them from applying.

Spain would not have anything to fear from a referendum in Melilla or Ceuta, but could not hold one whilst ignoring the referendum in Gibraltar. At the same time the nature of the territories concerned and the wishes of the population constitute a strong argument for Ceuta and Melilla remaining Spanish although contiguous with Moroccan territory outside the continent of Europe. A point of difference between the position of Gibraltar and that of the Spanish enclaves is that the Spanish territories were captured from the Moors before Morocco existed as an entity, whereas Gibraltar was captured and ceded by Spain as a nation. However, this cannot carry much weight against the wishes of the people concerned today. On this basis the argument for both places remaining as they are is a very strong one. Seas and rivers often form frontiers on account of the geographical convenience of such arrangements, but history has many instances of peoples stretching across seas as well as rivers.

PEOPLE VERSUS TERRITORIAL CLAIMS

Gibraltar, the Falkland Islands, Hong Kong and the Spanish Enclaves in North Africa are places where territorial claims conflict with the wishes of the present inhabitants. Hong Kong is different from the other three in that nearly the whole of the territory has to be returned to China in 1997, under the leasing arrangements, and this has been well known to the population for many years. Gibraltar is the only place in which a plebiscite has been held, but there can be little doubt in the other cases that the inhabitants would wish to continue in their present status. Britain's point of view is that the wishes of the people and their rights to self-determination as established by the United Nations Organisation should be paramount. Unfortunately Resolution

1514 (XV) of the UN does not give any precedence to considerations of self-determination under paragraph 2 or territorial integrity under paragraph 6, nor is there any definition of the circumstances to which territorial integrity apply. However, there was undoubtedly a piece of Spanish territory taken by Britain in 1704 and ceded in 1713 by treaty, and the UN has taken cogniscence of this. It has also called upon Britain and Spain to negotiate. The problem, therefore, becomes whether any way can be found of reconciling Spain's wish for territorial integrity and the Gibraltarians' wish for self-determination.

The earlier part of this chapter showed how small states can function with a high degree of independence, given goodwill by their neighbours. The case of Gibraltar differs in that it has a colonial status whereas the small states cited earlier have been established through the maintenance of independence from their neighbours. In the case of Andorra the mountainous terrain enabled a high degree of independence to be retained, whilst Monaco owes its position in some degree to the power of the Grimaldi family. If the colonial status of Gibraltar could be dismantled and if Britain and Spain could agree to rescind the Treaty of Utrecht in its application to Gibraltar, there is no reason why the Rock should not likewise become a small independent state in Europe. As frontiers within the EEC lose their importance, it might become possible for recognition to be given to Gibraltar as a territorial part of the EEC with its people free to run their own affairs as they wish. The British military presence could become more of a NATO presence on the southern flank of the alliance in a form acceptable to the government and people of Gibraltar. The withdrawal of the ceremonial guard from the frontier and the decision in 1989 to reduce the garrison have caused some dismay in Gibraltar on both economic and political grounds, but there are strong reasons for Britain reducing its profile on the Rock with a view to consolidating relations with Spain. With goodwill on both sides – and plenty of time – the present situation might be transformed and a solution reached which satisfies all parties concerned.

12
Gibraltar – Present and Future

Following the opening of the Spanish frontier in 1985 great changes have taken place in the commercial and economic life of Gibraltar, but it will take much more time for any substantial shift in attitudes towards Spain to occur amongst Gibraltarians. Since the opening of the frontier, both vehicles and pedestrians have generally had a fairly easy passage across the border and Gibraltarians have been able to visit relatives in Spain and go on other types of social visits. The island atmosphere of Gibraltar has changed, but there is still the same determination amongst Gibraltarians not to be dominated by Spain in any way. Fifteen years of a closed frontier have left their mark and time is needed to build up trust. This is something which must be recognised in Spain if progress is to be made. It may take at least until the end of the century for attitudes to change substantially, and even this will depend upon Spanish politicians adopting a much more friendly approach to Gibraltarians.

THE EVENTS OF 1988 AND THEIR EFFECTS

At the end of 1987 agreement was reached between Britain and Spain over a Spanish signature of the European Air Fares Agreement. A condition for the inclusion of Gibraltar Airport was the setting up of procedures for passengers to Spanish destinations to go straight to Spanish customs and immigration authorities with a similar procedure for travellers in the opposite direction. It was left to the Gibraltar government to accept or reject this. The year 1988 thus began with an imminent election for a new government and an unresolved question over the airport. The departure of Sir Joshua Hassan from the leadership of his party (GLP/AACR) was another major political factor. He had led his people through the difficult years of the closed frontier and had been closely associated with the Brussels Agreement which led to the opening of the frontier. He wisely avoided expressing views before handing over to Mr Canepa, who had been with him in the latest talks between Britain and Spain about the airport, but the general impression in Gibraltar was that the GLP/AACR was inclined to see the agreement as at least being worthy of further consideration. The opposition leader Mr Joe Bassano, on the other hand, was quite uninhibited in condemning the airport agreement and stating that Gibraltar should take no further part in discussions under the earlier Brussels Agreement. His election platform was that his party (the GSLP) would look after the interests of Gibraltarians and see that there were no concessions to Spain. The GSLP's ultimate victory at the polls in March was no doubt based on the party's attitude to the question of possible concessions to Spain over Gibraltar Airport.

Other issues in the election campaign of the GSLP included the setting up of a national bank, increased building of housing and achieving viability for the dockyard. The idea of having a national bank has been abandoned at least temporarily, but the government set to work with great energy on housing and saving the dockyard. In both these matters there has been a flexible approach in setting up joint ventures with private enterprise and in allowing building for sale to owner-occupiers as opposed to simply providing government housing for renting. At the northern end of the harbour a large reclamation scheme has been undertaken by a Dutch dredging company to provide land for housing. The dredger collects sand and shingle from the south of Europa Point and deposits this in the harbour. The possible effect on currents inside or outside the harbour remains to be seen, but one unexpected result has been the dredging up of dumped munitions and the Royal Engineers have had to be employed on disposing safely of some items. Before construction work can begin it will be necessary for a considerable amount of pile-driving to be undertaken.

Building construction also began in 1988 around Rosia Bay in an area of heritage sensitivity. In addition, work commenced on temporary units of accommodation in another area of historical interest west of the Line Wall. The site – formerly used as a

155

coach park – may eventually be released for some other use, but temporary housing often lasts for many years. The area was particularly suitable for coaches in that tourists from Spain could from here walk up steps into Cathedral Square and onto Main Street. Now the coaches have to park down in the harbour area and the entrance to Main Street is from the north-western end into Casemates Square.

Some progress was made during the first year of the GSLP government in reducing the losses of the dockyard. The dockyard has diversified to a certain extent, taking on for instance repair work for the Public Works Department, and financial losses have been substantially reduced. This is a question on which the government has to some extent staked its credibility after years of criticising its predecessors. The previous government had the advantage of £28 million made available by the UK government, which was largely spent on equipment, but a better result might have been achieved through less new equipment and better management. In particular more attention to industrial relations might have helped, but the disagreements between Gibrepair and the British-based management company Appledore was a source of much difficulty throughout the early years of transition from a naval to a commercial dockyard.

Whilst industrial relations in the dockyard may have improved after the advent of the GSLP to power, the government has encountered problems with the civil service. Considerable dissatisfaction has arisen from proposals for privatisation, even when this is into joint ventures or as in the case of the Tourist Office into a wholly-owned government agency. Senior civil servants have been reluctant to lose their security through joining a new type of organisation. The matter is quite a serious one in a small place where the competence and integrity of the civil service is so important. The civil service plays an important role in maintaining stability together with the judiciary, the Roman Catholic Church, other Christian churches and the Jewish Synagogue. The public's high regard for the civil service was in some respects demonstrated at the 1988 election when a party led by a former civil servant, Mr Pitaluga, entering the contest at a late stage obtained more than ten per cent of the votes. Mr Pitaluga's personal attributes played their part, but in the public eye he represented the great integrity of the civil service. The problem between the government and the civil service arises partly from uncertainty over how far privatisation or 'joint venturism' will go; the supply of electricity and the telecommunications industry are obvious contenders for such restructuring.

The attempt by the IRA to cause an explosion near a school and an old people's home in an effort to kill bandsmen of the Royal Anglian Regiment was in the forefront of news regarding Gibraltar for most of 1988. The plan nearly became a reality shortly before the election in March. It was foiled by the shooting and killing of two IRA men and one IRA woman near a petrol station not far from the airport. The coroner decided to hold an inquest. Later in the year the killing was held by a majority verdict to have been lawful, but the whole matter has been subject to much controversy, mostly outside Gibraltar. The persons shot and killed were unarmed at the time and it became clear later that it would have been possible to arrest them, but this was not known to the servicemen concerned in the shooting at the time they took action. A British television programme, *Death on the Rock*, was the source of some of the conflict over the matter. The British government asked the television company concerned to refrain from showing the programme until after the inquest, although it was not in contempt of court for it to be shown in Britain. The television company went ahead and showed the programme and the action of the company was vindicated in an inquiry after the inquest; there was also an award given later for excellence as documentary television.

In Gibraltar, however, there was much less inclination to argue over the ethics of the case; the predominant feeling was one of relief that the explosion had been prevented. It was suggested in the television programme that the coroner's court in Gibraltar was not the proper forum for an inquiry into the affair. The coroner was, however, properly exercising his prerogative and duty in ordering an inquest, and arrangements for security and other prelimary requirements as well as the inquest itself could hardly be faulted. The Spanish Government provided written information, but was not prepared to send any individuals to give verbal evidence.

Whilst the military in Gibraltar were engaged upon matters connected with the IRA attempted attack, the British Ministry of Defence was undertaking a review of requirements around the world. One result of this, announced early in 1989, was a decision to withdraw the infantry battalion from Gibraltar sometime after the beginning of 1990. From a defence point of view the possibilities would be an attack from outside the NATO alliance or some form of terrorist activity. With the airfield still under RAF control and the naval base being maintained, early reinforcement is a fairly simple matter and the expense of a permanent infantry battalion can hardly be justified. The news was however not well received in Gibraltar, as the removal of troops and their families will cause some economic loss and there was also a feeling of a loosening of British commitment to Gibraltar. A visit by Sir Geoffrey Howe, the British Foreign Minister, at the end of January went some way towards allaying fears in Gibraltar.

In May 1988 HRH The Duke of Gloucester visited Gibraltar in his capacity as President of the Friends of the Gibraltar Heritage Society. He visited many of the historic sites and familiarised himself with work being done to preserve them. It had been hoped that he would be able to inaugurate the taking over of the Garrison Library by the Gibraltar Heritage Trust, but in the absence of agreement between all the parties concerned this had to remain in abeyance.

Financial matters affecting Gibraltar came to the forefront in the middle of 1988 when investors in Barlow Clowes International based in Gibraltar found their shareholdings almost valueless through the company going into liquidation. It will probably be several years before the full results of this are known and the matter has become the subject of both criminal and civil litigation. The liquidation of the company gave Gibraltar some unwanted publicity, but the UK and other countries are also affected by the failure of

Barlow Clowes companies, so it is by no means a wholly Gibraltarian affair.

THE AIRPORT

The airport lies at the north end of the Rock on the edge of the territory, but is central to much of the life of Gibraltar. During the fifteen years of the closed frontier – often known as the fifteenth siege – the airport was Gibraltar's lifeline with the outside world. The GSLP's rejection in 1988 of joint use by Spain can be expected to have long-term effects. Without Spanish co-operation the Gibraltar airline (GB Airways) cannot fly to European destinations other than Britain. Lack of co-operation also prevents extension of the runway, which is not long enough for fully-loaded aircraft larger than the Boeing 737 presently in use.

GB Airways provides about twenty flights each week between Britain and Gibraltar varying according to the season. These are nearly all from Gatwick, but Manchester is also served. The airline forms part of the Bland Group which was founded in 1810 as a shipping agency. The group of companies has been associated with the Gaggero family for many years; the present chairman is the fifth generation of the family in the business and his son is director of the airline. Other interests of the Bland Group include the Rock Hotel, a travel agency and the cable car.

During the years of the closed frontier GB Airways operated daily services to Tangier with a Viscount aircraft, but this has now been retired from service. It is to be replaced with a Trislander, so that the service can be resumed and possibly extended to Casablanca. There are also plans to operate services to European destinations provided problems over the exclusion of Gibraltar Airport from the European Air Fares Agreement can be overcome.

There are some apparent contradictions in the GSLP government's thinking over the airport. The idea of joint Spanish use was still firmly rejected at the beginning of 1989, but plans were being considered for a new airport to the east of the Rock on reclaimed land or a possible extension to the west; in either case Spanish co-operation would be necessary. Another problem

over increasing the capacity of the airport is the fact that the road
to Spain and the airport buildings crosses the runway near its
western end. If there were much greater use of the airport, road
traffic problems would be aggravated beyond an acceptable level.
The possibility of building a road tunnel has been mooted, but
this would be a massive engineering undertaking.

At the time of writing, the first year in office of the GSLP
has perhaps resulted in some changes in thinking on the question
of co-operation with Spain. It is clear that some move in this
direction is economically desirable, but there is an understand-
able Gibraltarian insistence on being accepted by Spaniards on
a basis of equality; this applies to practically all Gibraltarians
whatever their political inclinations.

THE NEED FOR TIME

Time and much patience are needed to resolve present differences
over the Rock – the home of the Gibraltarians. They have a right,
that can hardly be doubted, to be regarded as a people. Small in
numbers though they are, they have a contribution to make to the
EEC and to Europe as a whole. Progress has been made since the
Lisbon Agreement of 1980 in achieving a better understanding
between Britain and Spain over Gibraltar and there are signs of a
greater acceptance by Spanish governments that they must take
account of the wishes of the Gibraltarians. There is, however,
a need for much more time for a proper mutual understanding
to develop between all three parties. The years of a closed
frontier cannot be erased from the minds of Gibraltarians and
the question is largely one of building up trust between parties
with different attitudes and interests. This particularly applies
between the Spanish government and the Gibraltarians.

The attitudes of the three parties concerned – Britain, Spain
and the Gibraltarians – can be summarised as follows. Britain
is committed to continuing in its present role as long as the
Gibraltarians wish for it. At the same time Britain does not
want relations with Spain soured by a dispute over Gibraltar
and thus Britain has an interest in keeping the problem in the
background as far as possible. Spain, on the other hand, wishes
to recover the Rock to satisfy its national pride and, therefore,

brings this emotive issue to the forefront from time to time; the dispute over Gibraltar Airport at the end of 1987 was one example of this. The matter was raised in relation to Spanish claims to sovereignty over the isthmus, which was not covered by the terms of the Treaty of Utrecht. This caused Gibraltarians to react with disquiet and distrust as is the case whenever the question of Spanish sovereignty arises. Gibraltarians do not want any change in their status in relation to Spain and wish to manage their own affairs under the British sovereignty which they have experienced for nearly three centuries.

Spain is the country seeking change in status for Gibraltar, but this can only be achieved by gaining the trust of Gibraltarians. This will only happen when Spain recognises the right of Gibraltarians to self-determination and to become an independent state if they wish. This would be a difficult line for any Spanish government to take after many years of governments having fostered the belief amongst Spaniards that the Rock should be under Spanish sovereignty. A start might be made by leaving the word 'sovereignty' out of statements about the Rock. The term breeds emotional feeling without providing clarity of meaning, particularly when statements are made suggesting that Spain simply wants the Rock but will leave Gibraltarians to run their own affairs. Gibraltarians do not believe that this could happen, but on the other hand it is by no means impossible that an independent Gibraltar could eventually wish to join Spain. Thus supporting Gibraltarian self-determination and moves towards independence might be the approach which in time could bring Spain the jewel which it feels it has lost.

The sting of the thorn of British sovereignty might also be removed by a decolonisation process leading to independence. Gibraltarians may well regard this as an advocacy of 'osmosis', but this is another emotive term which like 'sovereignty' could well be dropped. Moves towards a truly European community of nations should in time lead to a lessening use of both terms. The greatest need is for friendship between Spain and Gibraltar to be developed. The process should be a mutual one, but Spain as a large country can best take the initiative. At the same time both British and Gibraltarian people have to try to understand

Spanish feelings over the Rock. From a Spanish angle, Gibraltar stands as a monument to defeats and occupation first by the Moors and then by the British. Britain has suffered many defeats in its history, from the Battle of Hastings to the fall of Singapore, but the Normans were absorbed into British society and Singapore was recovered before becoming independent with strong British ties. There is no monument to these defeats on the British mainland. Times change, and the gradual loosening of frontiers in the EEC may well make the issue of Gibraltar's separateness far less significant. There is no need for haste.

In the meantime within the small area of the Rock there is a rich natural and historical heritage with a contribution to make as a small and in some ways unique place. It contains an industrious people who can make their own living without having to rely on outside help. The people have a culture drawn from many outside influences and a tolerance of diverse ways not always found in Europe or elsewhere. With a Mediterranean warmth, charm and courtesy, Gibraltarians are most welcoming to visitors and this openness has helped cultivate their flourishing tourist industry. From a tourist angle Gibraltar is complementary to the Costa del Sol in Spain; longer stretches of sandy beach can be found in Spain, but Gibraltar provides a wealth of natural, historical and human interest within a small area. For instance, at the northern end of the Rock there are the Moorish Castle, the Galleries and batteries of the Great Siege and also War War II defences all within a short walking distance of each other. About two miles away at the southern end of the Rock can be found a mixed *maquis* type of vegetation with good observation points for migratory birds. Between these two ends of the Rock, the cable car provides a route from the colourful Alameda Gardens to the Apes Den Station and then on to views from the top westwards through the Straits and eastwards into the Mediterranean. Gibraltar and its people are well worth a visit.

APPENDIX 1

Some Notable Dates

Date	Event
711	Tarik's Moorish forces land without opposition in April, beginning their invasion of Spain
1160	Fortification of Gibraltar ordered by Al-Mu'mim. The Moorish Wall dates from about this time.
1309	*First Siege.* Alonso Peres de Guzman takes Gibraltar after a siege of one month.
1316	*Second Siege.* Moorish attempt at recapture fails.
1333	*Third Siege.* Vasco Perez surrenders to Moorish forces after a siege of four months.
1333	*Fourth Siege.* Alfonso XI tries to recapture the Rock but fails.
1349–50	*Fifth Siege.* Alfonso XI makes another attempt to drive out the Moors, but the effort ends in his death of plague in March 1350.
1411	*Sixth Siege.* The Rock taken by forces of the Gran adian Moorish kingdom from the kingdom of Fez.
1436	*Seventh Siege.* Henry de Guzman, Count of Niebla, fails to capture the Rock and is killed in the attempt.
1462	*Eighth Siege.* Alonso de Arcos initiates an attack and is joined by other Spanish forces before Gibraltar is captured in the name of the Duke of Medina in August. Later in the year the Crown of Spain annexes it, the Duke giving it up under protest.
1466–67	*Ninth Siege.* Henry de Guzman, son of the Duke of Medina, captures the Rock after a siege of fifteen months.
1502	Gibraltar placed under the Crown of Spain by Isabella, with agreement of the third Duke of Medina.
1506	*Tenth Siege.* Third Duke of Medina imposes a blockade, but abandons it without serious fighting.

1540	Turkish pirates land and pillage, taking captives away with them. Most of the captives saved by a Spanish naval squadron.
1624	Philip IV of Spain visits Gibraltar, and sets in progress many improvements to the defences.
1693	Some ships of a British convoy escorted by Admiral Rooke on the way to Mediterranean ports shelter in Gibraltar after being scattered by a French attack.
1704	*Eleventh Siege.* British fleet under Admiral Rooke and British and Dutch land forces under Prince George of Hesse capture Gibraltar on 4 August in name of King Charles III of Spain after an attack lasting a few days.
1704–05	*Twelfth Siege.* Forces supporting Philip V of Spain begin an attack on the Rock in October 1704. The siege continues until April 1705, but is unsuccessful.
1713	Spain cedes Gibraltar to Britain by Article X of the Treaty of Utrecht.
1727	*Thirteenth Siege.* Spanish and French attempt made to recapture Gibraltar by a siege begun in February and lasting about five months before hostilities are suspended.
1779–83	*Fourteenth Siege.* Spanish and French forces besiege the Rock from June 1779 until February 1783. Relieving fleets arrive in 1780, 1781 and 1782. A sortie is made in November 1781 and a heavy bombardment by besieging forces in September 1782.
1789–1815	French Revolution, followed by the Napoleonic Wars. After a decline in trade following the French Revolution Gibraltar develops as an entrepôt port for British ships excluded from other European ports. Nelson's victory at Trafalgar in 1805 removes the threat of a siege of Gibraltar. The *Victory*, with Nelson's body on board, comes to Rosia Bay a few days after the battle.
1830	Fifth Charter of Justice sets up Supreme Court, the first move towards civil government.
1865	Sanitary Commissioners appointed.

1869	Suez Canal opened.
1893	Work begun on South Mole, marking the start of the building of the naval harbour of 440 acres (178 hectares), completed by 1905.
1914–18	*World War I.* Gibraltar used for examination for contraband, convoy collection and anti-submarine operations.
1921	City Council elections held, marking the beginning of moves to representative government.
1936–39	Spanish Civil War. Nationalist troops from Morocco land at Algeciras and elsewhere in July 1936. War ends in April 1939.
1939–45	*World War II.* Gibraltar again used for convoy collection and as base for anti-submarine operations. It is main base for the launching of the British and American campaign in North Africa.
1950	First Legislative Council established.
1954	Spanish consul withdrawn and restrictions begun on crossing the frontier at La Linea.
1969	Spanish frontier closes at La Linea and ferry to Algeciras withdrawn. Telephone links with Spain cut.
1980	Lisbon Agreement on Anglo-Spanish approach to Gibraltar question following Spain's return to democracy after Franco's death in 1975.
1982	Limited re-opening of frontier to pedestrians in December.
1984	Brussels Agreement in December on re-opening frontier.
1985	Frontier fully re-opened in February.

Article X of
The Treaty of Utrecht

The Catholic King does hereby, for himself, his heirs and successors, yield to the Crown of Great Britain the full and entire propriety of the town and castle of Gibraltar, together with the port, fortifications and forts thereunto belonging; and he gives up the said propriety to be held and enjoyed absolutely with all manner of right for ever, without any exception or impediment whatsoever. But that abuses and frauds may be avoided by importing any kind of goods, the Catholic King wills and takes it to be understood that the above-named propriety be yielded to Great Britain without any territorial jurisdiction, and without any open communication by land with the country round about. Yet whereas the communication by sea with the coast of Spain may not at all times be safe or open, and thereby it may happen that the garrison and other inhabitants of Gibraltar may be brought to great straits; and as it is the intention of the Catholic King, only the fraudulent importation of goods should, as is above said, be hindered by an inland communication, it is therefore provided that in such cases it may be lawful to purchase, for ready money, in the neighbouring territories of Spain, provisions and other things necessary for the use of the garrison, the inhabitants and the ships which lie in the harbour. But if any goods be found imported by Gibraltar, either by way of barter for purchasing provisions, or under any other pretence, the same shall be confiscated, and complaint being made thereof, those persons who have acted contrary to the faith of this country, shall be severely punished. And Her Britannic Majesty at the request of the Catholic King, does consent and agree, that no leave shall be given under any pretence whatsoever, either to Jews or Moors, to reside or have their dwellings in the said town of Gibraltar; and that no refuge or shelter shall be allowed to any

Moorish ships of war in the harbour of the said town, whereby the communication between Spain and Ceuta may be obstructed, or the coasts of Spain be infested by the excursions of the Moors. But whereas treaties of friendship and a liberty and intercourse of commerce are between the British and certain territories situate on the coast of Africa, it is always to be understood, that the British subjects cannot refuse the Moors and their ships entry into the port of Gibraltar purely upon the account of merchandising. Her Majesty the Queen of Great Britain does further promise, that the free exercise of their religion shall be indulged to the Roman Catholic inhabitants of the aforesaid town. And in case it shall hereafter seem meet to the Crown of Great Britain to grant, sell, or by any means to alienate therefrom the propriety of the said town of Gibraltar, it is hereby agreed, and concluded, that the preference of having the same shall always be given to the Crown of Spain before any others.

APPENDIX 3

SCHEMATIC DIAGRAM SHOWING
ARRANGEMENT OF PRODUCTION, STORAGE
AND SUPPLY OF GIBRALTAR'S POTABLE
WATER SYSTEM.

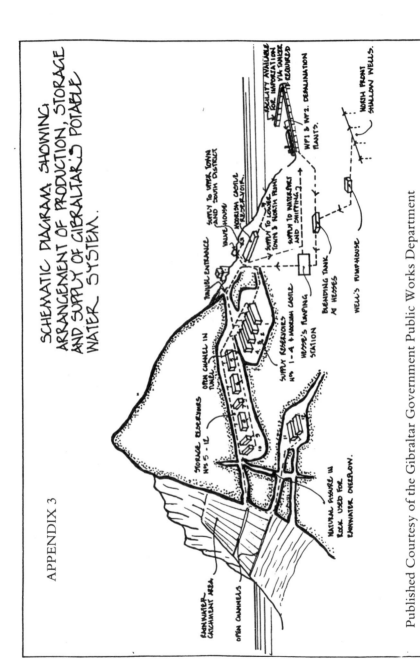

Published Courtesy of the Gibraltar Government Public Works Department

Bibliography

ANDREWS, ALLEN. *Proud Fortress*

BAILEY, SIR EDWARD. 'Gibraltar and the Northern Rif', *Quarterly Journal of the Geological Society of London*, Vol 108 (1952)

BENADY, TITO. *Guide-book to Gibraltar* (Gibraltar 1985)

BERNADY DE FRANCOISE. *Princes of Monaco* (1961)

BRADFORD, EARLE. *Gibraltar* (1971)

CONN, S. *Gibraltar in British Diplomacy in the Eighteenth Century* (Yale 1942)

CORTES, J.E., FINLAYSON, J.C., MOSQUERA, M.A., GARCIA, E.F.J. *The Birds of Gibraltar* (Gibraltar 1980)

DEANE, SHIRLEY. *The Road to Andorra* (1960)

DENNIS, PHILIP. *Gibraltar* (Newton Abbot 1977)

DIETZ, PETER. *Garrison – Ten British Garrison Towns* (1986)

DRINKWATER, JOHN. *A History of the Late Siege of Gibraltar* (1785)

DUNCAN, FRANCIS. *History of the Royal Artillery*

ELLICOTT, D.M. and J.T. *An Ornament to the Almeida* (Portsmouth 1950)

ELLICOTT, DOROTHY. 'Tarik's Hill', *Commonwealth and Empire Annual* (1953)

—*Bastion against Aggression* (Gibraltar 1968)

—*Our Gibraltar* (Gibraltar 1975)

—*Gibraltar's Royal Governor* (Gibraltar 1981)

FANSHAWE, ADMIRAL SIR EDWARD. *Sir Hew Dalrymple at Gibraltar*

FIELD, HENRY. *Gibraltar*

FISHER, JAMES. *Watching Birds* (1974)

FOREIGN AND COLONIAL OFFICE. *Gibraltar: Recent differences with Spain (HMSO 1965)*.

—*Talks with Spain* (HMSO 1966)

—*Further Documents (HMSO 1967 and HMSO 1968)*

GARCIA, RICHARD. *Anecdotes and Stories about the Gibraltar Post Office 1886–1985*

GARDINER, SIR ROBERT. *Report to Lord Palmerston*

GIBRALTAR GARRISON LIBRARY. *Ups and Downs of the Royal Calpe Hunt* (Gibraltar 1912)

—*Wild Flowers of Gibraltar and the Neighbourhood* (Gibraltar 1968)

GIBRALTAR GOVERNMENT. *Annual Reports* (1957–72)

—*Census Reports* (1970 & 81)

—*Annual Digests of Statistics*

GONZALES, A. *History of the Gibraltar Dockyard*, Journal of the Gibraltar Society, Vol 1 (1930), 26–52

HILLS, GEORGE *Franco* (1967)

—*Rock of Contention* (1974)

HOFFMANN, FRITZ L. and OLGA MINGO. *Sovereignty in Dispute The Falklands/Malvinas* 1493–1982 (1984)

HOLDSWORTH, SIR WILLIAM, *A History of English Law* (1956 Edition)

HONG KONG GOVERNMENT INFORMATION SERVICES. *Hong Kong* (1987)

HORT, R. *The Rock* (1839)

HOWES, DR H.W. *The Gibraltarians* (1951)

HUGHES, B.P. *British Smooth Bore Artillery*

IRBY, HOWARD L. *Ornithology of the Straits of Gibraltar*

JACKSON, SIR WILLIAM G.F. *The Rock of the Gibraltarians* (1987)

JAMES, COLONEL THOMAS. *History of the Herculean Straits* (1771)

JONES, MAURICE, *History of Coast Artillery in the British Army*

KENYON, MAJOR GENERAL E.R. *Gibraltar under Moor, Spaniard and Briton* (1911)

LAWRENCE, MIKE. *The Wild Dolphins of Gibraltar* (Gibraltar 1986)

LAWSON, DON. *The Lion and the Rock* (Gibraltar 1986)

LUDWIG, EMIL. *The Mediterranean*

MANN, J.H. *Gibraltar and its Sieges* (1870)

MORRIS, JAN. *Hong Kong* (1987)

NAGEL'S TRAVEL GUIDE. *Six Little States of Europe* (1961)

OVE ARUP and Partners. *Gibraltar Groundwater Survey* (1971)

BIBLIOGRAPHY

OWEN, CHARLES. *The Maltese Islands* (Newton Abbot 1969)

PACK, S.W.C. *Sea Power in the Mediterranean* (1971)

PALAO, GEORGE. *The Guns and Towers of Gibraltar* (Gibraltar 1975)

PALMER, TERRY. *Discover Gibraltar* (1987)

PERL, RAPHAEL. *The Falkland Islands Dispute in International Law and Politics* (1984)

REZETTE, ROBERT. *The Spanish Enclaves in Morocco* (Paris 1976)

RUSSELL, JACK. *Gibraltar Besieged* (1965)

RYAN, E.F.E. *Something about Gibraltar* (1943)

SAYER, CAPTAIN. *History of Gibraltar* (1862)

SPANISH GOVERNMENT. *The Spanish Red Book* (Madrid 1965)

—*Negotiations on Gibraltar* (Madrid 1968)

—*Spain's Point of View* (Madrid 1974)

STEWART, JOHN D. *Gibraltar the Keystone* (1967)

STRANGE, IAN J. *The Falkland Islands* (3rd Edition) (Newton Abbot 1983)

TAYLOR, ERNEST R. *Padre Brown of Gibraltar*

TUKE, LT. COLONEL A.J.S. *Birds of Southern Spain and Gibraltar*

WILSON, W.H. 'Tunnelling on the Rock', *Institute of Mining and Metallurgy Journal* (Vol 55 [1945–6], 193–269)

Acknowledgements

It is impracticable to list all the sources of information for this book, but the main works of reference are listed in the bibliography. Many individuals and organisations in Gibraltar, including the Chief Ministers of present and past governments, the Gibraltar Tourist Office (now incorporated in the new Gibraltar Information Bureau), other government departments and the Garrison Library have given help. The Library is temporarily closed at the time of writing but it is inconceivable that something will not be done to overcome its financial difficulties. Its archives include unpublished sources of information as well as the published ones listed in the bibliography and mention should be made of Mrs Huart's unique knowledge of what is there. She has always been most helpful to the author in finding the less well known sources of information to supplement items such as *Gibraltar Chronicles* going back for over 180 years and *Gibraltar Directories* going back to 1881; these were published annually in the years before World War II.

In the United Kingdom help has been obtained from the Royal Commonwealth Society Library, the Henley Town Library, the Foreign Office, the Spanish Embassy and many other organisations and persons. Amongst individuals who have helped mention must be made of Tito Benady and Michael Brufal, both of whom have much knowledge of Gibraltar. The photographs have kindly been provided by the persons named, or in most cases by the Gibraltar Tourist Office (GTO).

In recent years the author has made frequent visits to Gibraltar, his interest having been kindled in earlier years through being a son of army parents stationed there. For about fifteen years Joe and Sylvia Ballantine have provided a friendly atmosphere in which many ideas have been obtained, both in their home and elsewhere, including the naval establishments of *HMS Rooke* and *HMS Calpe*. Finally, thanks are due to Joy Wallbank for turning untidy pages into a typescript intelligible to the publishers.

Index